GRACE

from

GRIT

Finding Calm Amidst the Chaos of Motherhood

Michelle Collins Page

I dedicate this book to...

My Heavenly Father, for this amazing life.

My husband, Pete, for his unconditional love.

Pete, Patrick, Nori, and daughter-in-law, Elena, for the privilege of being called mom.

My Mother's Gathering support group, whose light, love, and hope gave me the courage to share my journey.

"Angel" by Nori Page

"For I know the plans I have for you," declares the Lord, "plans to prosper you and not to harm you, plans to give you hope and a future. Then you will call on me and come and pray to me, and I will listen to you."-- Jeremiah 29:11-12

TABLE OF CONTENTS

Motherhood and Oysters

The late humorist Erma Bombeck once wrote, "Giving birth is little more than a set of muscular contractions granting passage of a child. Then the mother is born." The discomfort of delivering life is temporary, but the byproduct delivers a lifetime of joy. However, when circumstances rob us of our hopes and dreams for our children, labor pains pale in comparison to the emotional trauma we endure. This book is for mothers who have not only celebrated motherhood's magic but also suffered its heartbreaking heaviness.

As a new author, creating a title that would reach my intended audience took work. Finding a few words that could grab a reader's attention, convey the book's purpose, and set the tone for the following chapters proved daunting. Finally, it occurred to me that oysters and mothers have a lot in common.

My husband and I live on a barrier island off the coast of Charleston, South Carolina. Fresh seafood is abundant, and we especially look forward to the "R" months when oysters are plentiful. Whether raw or roasted, those briny mollusks topped with cocktail sauce, a dollop of horseradish, and a squeeze of lemon are heaven on a cracker. And they bear uncanny similarities to mothers.

For instance, you can search the world but never find two identical oysters or mothers.

Oysters and motherhood are an acquired taste. They're not for everyone.

The oyster shell is resilient, protecting the delicate morsel inside, just as mothers safeguard their children.

Mothers nourish their children physically, emotionally, and spiritually in the same way oysters provide vitamins and nutrients to the consumer.

Oysters filter 1.3 gallons of water per hour, helping maintain the balance of their ecosystem. Mothers also provide filters for their children, striving to create the delicate balance of too much, too little, bad out, and good in. Lastly, oysters use irritants- a piece of sand, grit, or shell- to produce a beautiful pearl. It can take two to ten years, but the result is worth the wait. One would be hard-pressed to find a mother who has not encountered impediments and aggravations along their long, child-rearing journey. But these irritants often form the people that God intended them to be. *Grace from Grit* explores how we can manage our lives with grace while negotiating the grit and grind of motherhood.

I am not, if you wonder, qualified to create a spiritual guide for mothers. But I have lived experiences with which the reader may commiserate, including infertility, premature births, substance abuse, and mental illness. We live in a social media bubble that emphasizes the highlight reels of our lives, where we hesitate to reveal the blooper clips. My goal is to share my textured motherhood journey within the safe confines of these pages and create a relationship with the reader who can whisper silently, "Me, too."

Grace from Grit is divided into three parts. Grit, where we encounter the sucker punch of uncertainty; Grind, how we navigate the journey; and Grace, when we find acceptance and hope. Each chapter begins with a quote from a children's book addressing the topic. As a former kindergarten teacher, I always considered the lessons taught in children's literature relevant to adulthood.

Motherhood can be messy, but there is always hope when we rely entirely on the one who made us mothers. As Bombeck advised, *"A child needs your love most when he deserves it least."* We give them that love when we trust Him to use the grit of their lives to create people with grace, character, and humility.

PETE AND ELENA'S WEDDING 9/2/2022

grit

/grit/

noun

1. small loose particles of stone or sand.
   "she had a bit of grit in her eye."

2. courage and resolve; strength of character.
   "he displayed the true grit of the navy pilot."

In the movie *True Grit,* teenager Mattie Ross enlists the assistance of Rooster Cogburn to find her father's killer. Rooster doubts that Mattie possesses enough backbone and resilience to complete this mission, but she soon proves him wrong. Mattie embodies true grit.

The conveniences of modern society have practically eliminated the necessity for resourcefulness and tenacity. We ride share and order takeout. Texts and emails have replaced walks to the mailbox. Loose and leisurely clothing takes precedence over dressing to impress.

But there are no shortcuts or quick fixes for motherhood. It is a season of endurance. The physical pain of giving birth marks the beginning of emotional fluctuations, sleeplessness, financial strain, and uncertainty. It is a journey rife with precious moments but sometimes unspeakable pain.

My quest just to become a mother required grit. Ten years of infertility and the birth of very premature twins presented the first of many challenges. Navigating their life-threatening illnesses and severe injuries left me physically and emotionally drained. Faith became my lifeline.

Disappointment and motherhood are a package deal, no matter how well one performs those maternal duties. But Chris Morris reminds us that "Grit is having the courage to push through, no matter what the obstacles are, because it's worth it." And it is so worth it.

Praying for Fishhooks

"Then Miss Watson, she took me in the closet and prayed, but nothing come of it. She told me to pray every day, and whatever I asked for, I would get it. But it warn't so."

The Adventures of Huckleberry Finn by Mark Twain

When Miss Watson advised Huck to pray for anything, and he would get it, he prayed for fishhooks. He did manage to snag a fishing line, but no hooks. After he tried three more times with no luck, he asked Miss Watson to pray for him. She calls him a fool, but Huck never understands why.

Mark Twain had strong opinions about religion, which he imparted to some of his characters. He was not an atheist, but he was also not easily swayed by religious propaganda or sermons. The Widow and Miss Watson, guardians of Huck Finn until his drunken Pap arrived to take custody of him, were Christians but conveyed their beliefs differently. Miss Watson's strict adherence to scripture differed in tone from the Widow's compassionate explanations. When Miss Watson advised Huck that God answers all prayers, the Widow clarified that He answers with spiritual gifts, not material things.

I hold two college degrees: a B.S. in Business/Finance from the University of South Carolina and a Master of Arts in Teaching from the College of Charleston. Despite being "highly educated," as some would say, my employment history and earning potential have been erratic. Those beautifully framed diplomas hanging on my wall didn't hold sway when my chosen fields of study failed to synchronize with my skill set and timing.

My first job out of college quickly convinced me that banking was about as exciting as watching paint dry. Another drawback of this profession was the necessity of wearing hosiery. If you've ever experienced the summer humidity of Charleston, South Carolina, you can understand how sweaty legs encased in nylon could deter lofty aspirations in this industry. I also do not enjoy climbing ladders, especially the corporate ones built with rungs of monotony and Banker

Barbie wardrobe requirements. My flip-flops and fancy-free lifestyle did not mesh with the proper demands of this profession.

So, I embarked on earning a teaching degree at the ripe old age of thirty and committed to a new career path, paving the way to a well-paying job with benefits where I could utilize my creativity while inspiring young generations, as the Army recruiting slogan goes, "to be all that they can be." (If you are a teacher, you are most likely laughing your badonkadonk off right now.) It turns out that an advanced degree with zero, zip, nada experience presents a challenge when competing with peppy, fresh-out-of-college young adults. No one wants to hire a thirty-something-year-old whose naivete' considers "self-paced" an approach to drinking alcohol rather than a method of instruction.

I finally settled for a job teaching four-year-olds at my church's preschool. By that time, my children were in school, two of them where I worked, so I accepted my fate, and life went on.

Eventually, the job of my dreams became available: A kindergarten position at the school two miles from my house and where all three of my children would attend. A school that claims a beach on the Atlantic Ocean as its backyard. A neighborhood school where many students walk, ride bikes, or parents chauffeur them in golf carts. I harbored visions of the four of us traveling to school/work in our golf cart and cavorting on the beach afterward.

I suffered a double whammy of disappointment when not only did I not get the job, but the position went to the 5K teacher across the hall from me. My preschool rubbed some salt into my self-esteem wounds when they asked me to fill her vacancy.

While it wasn't the salary-job-with-benefits I hoped for (cue laughter again from teachers), I prayerfully considered this offer and eventually committed, unaware that the next fifteen years would be some of the most fulfilling times of my life. God did not say no to my prayers; he rerouted them to a path better suited for His purpose. I could not share stories about His abundant love in a public school setting. Instead of identifying as the poster child of unanswered prayers, this redirection allowed me to impact not only children's educations but their spiritual lives as well.

The Bible teems with people who experienced the agony of unanswered prayers, only to have them realized in unexpected or untimely ways. Hannah cried so often and intensely for a child that Eli, a priest, accused her of being drunk. But when Hannah explained her situation, she promised Eli that she would give her child to God if she could conceive. When Samuel was born, she made good on that promise. (1 Samuel 1:2-2:21)

Why did it take so long for God to grant Hannah's wishes? Eli raised Samuel in the temple, and over time, his honesty and dedication to God earned him the titles of prophet and judge. These opportunities would not have been available if he had been born sooner. As the saying goes, timing is everything. And God's is perfect.

My husband and I waited ten long years for a child, stunted by infertility. Like Hannah, God ignored my prayers, or so I thought. During this same period of my life, I experienced mental health struggles that strained the stability of our marriage and relationships with friends and family. Only now do I understand that God was not saying no to my quest for a child, but He was synchronizing it with the restoration of my health so that I could manage the responsibilities of motherhood.

During my thirty-one years of being a mom, there have been many times I felt God was ignoring my prayers for my children. As my pleas for help became louder, His voice became quieter, threatening my belief that He even existed. The gift of hindsight now affords me the understanding that He was listening, but my suggestions did not align with His master plan. Now some of the most painful pieces of their life puzzles are being utilized in ways I could not understand while they were evolving.

We all grapple with prayers that go unanswered. But God is a loving God, and there are reasons that He does not answer specific requests, choosing redirection over rejection. He does not punish us but prepares us for a chance to bring greater glory to Him through new adventures. In the words of Warren Wiersbe,[1] "God is more interested in our character than our comfort."

Whether praying for fishhooks, a job, or a child, God will only grant our petitions if they align with His will. And if "you ask and do not receive, because you ask with wrong motives, so that you may spend it on your pleasures," rest assured that what God does deliver will bring you spiritual fulfillment. (James 4:3)

---

[1] Weirsbe, Warren W. *Famous Unanswered Prayers.* Lincoln, Nebraska: Back to the Bible, 1986.

My career choices have not been lucrative in a monetary sense, but my blessings have made me rich beyond measure. I have a loving husband, three amazing children, and a new daughter-in-law. Like Huck, my "fishhooks" never materialized, but my prayers were answered beyond what those diplomas could ever offer.

"Wetting a Fishhook"

WORRY
Worrying is a Waste of Time

"Wemberly worried about everything. Big things, little things, and things in between."

Wemberly Worried by Kevin Henkes

Wemberly was a worrier of the worst kind. She worried about spilling her juice. She worried that she would shrink when taking a bath. She even worried that there were snakes in the radiator. She worried morning, noon, and night. "Worry, worry, worry," her family said. "Too much worry." But Wemberly was most worried about her first day of school. Her worries dissipated when she met a fellow worry wart and soon realized that school is too much fun to waste time worrying.

According to Vocabulary.com, the word worry comes from the Old English origin *wyrgan*, which means "to strangle." In his book *Worry*, Dr. Hallowell states that one in four Americans will meet the criteria for anxiety disorder at some point in their lifetime, and over half of them are chronic worriers.[2] It would be interesting to know how many of these are mothers.

My mom and her sister were inseparable from birth. Lovingly known as "The Sistas" at their church and in their neighborhood, you rarely saw one without the other. They wore hearts of gold on their sleeves and were the first to reach out in times of crisis with casseroles, hugs, and prayers.

While compassionately synchronized, they prioritized other worries differently. Aunt Martha's dish towels, organized by color and use, demonstrated her domesticity. Always fashionably dressed and accessorized, Mom preferred conviviality over cleaning any day of the week, and her clothing hung in rainbow hues. A malfunctioning iron would throw a kink in Aunt Martha's carefully scheduled day, while Mom's frequently misplaced calendar caused her to mourn missed social engagements. They both worried, but one panicked about the practical, while the other fretted over the fanciful.

[2] Hallowell, Edward, M.D. *Worry: Hope and Help for a Common Condition.* New York City: Ballentine Books, 1998.

Mary and Martha had such a relationship. While Martha scurried to prepare a feast for Jesus and his friends, Mary sat at his feet, worshipping him. When Martha complained to Jesus that her sister was shirking her duties in the preparation, he gently corrected her by stating that "Mary has chosen the better part." (Luke 10:42)

There is an old proverb that reminds us that "worrying is like sitting in a rocking chair; it gives you something to do, but it doesn't get you anywhere." Worrying not only does not prevent something from happening, but it can deter one from leading a fulfilling life. As Mark Twain once said, "I have spent most of my life worrying about things that have never happened."

More scientifically explained, Cornell University conducted a study and found that 85% of the things that people worry about never come to fruition. Furthermore, 79% of the 15% who did face a crisis managed it better than they thought they could have. The study concluded that 97% of the worrying was unnecessary.[3] In the words of Sarah Ban Breathnach, "Worrying is a great thief of time."[4]

As comforting as these statistics are on paper, try telling that to any mother you have ever met. Mothers' hearts beat in synchronization with their children, and we have heart palpitations and panic attacks to prove it. I am willing to bet that very few mothers have never done "breathing checks" on their babies in the middle of the night.

For two and a half months of my twin's lives, this was unnecessary. Born three months early, they were monitored 24/7. During their hospitalization, I could find out their oxygen saturation rate, their weight, and how many ounces of formula they consumed at any moment. Being privy to this information was also a disadvantage. There was always a direct correlation between my mood and the nurse's morning report. I was Wemberly the Worrier on steroids. Those babies turned 29 this year, so I can happily state that I am a proud member of the Cornell 97% statistic.

Matthew 6:34 tells us this: "Therefore do not worry about tomorrow, for tomorrow will worry about itself. Each day has enough trouble of its own." Worry is a snake bite whose venom threatens to

---

[3] Holman, Richard. "Why We Should Worry Less." *Richard Holman,* 9 May 2023.

[4] Breathnach, Sarah Ban. *Simple Abundance: A Daybook of Comfort and Joy.* New York City: Warner Publishing, 1995.

extinguish hope. Prayer is the antidote. And as the author Tim Keller states, it "brings a comfort and rest that nothing else can bring."

Aunt Martha and Mom

FRUSTRATION
Freedom from Frustration

*"Yet he wouldn't...just couldn't...let anything go...
Which made his frustration continue to grow."*

The Very Frustrated Monster by Andi Green

Twitch gets frustrated about everything, from ill-fitting gym shorts to missing the school bus. He even complains because the sun is too bright. When he finds his situation unchangeable, he blames his friends. He gains a new perspective when he witnesses a squirrel dropping and retrieving nuts from the ground, then climbing back up the tree only to do it again. He realizes that if the squirrel is not frustrated with this mindless task, why should he?

Frustration is often the result of our inability to change a circumstance or a person to suit us. Habits are so ingrained that only diligent and conscientious efforts will eradicate them. Patterns repeat ad nauseam, frustration growing with each occurrence. If you are married or have children, you know of which I speak.

My husband and I just celebrated our 41st wedding anniversary. Over time, we have both developed idiosyncrasies that are downright irritating to each other. By nature, he has always been methodical, minimal, and neat; on the contrary, my favorite activities include multi-tasking and hoarding. He walks at a leisurely pace; I "stroll" like my hair has caught on fire. His tool shed is organized by usage and labeled appropriately; my craft room (or "crap" room as he refers to it) could pass as the aftermath of the apocalypse. For forty-one years, we have tolerated each other's differences, and neither one of us has the energy nor motivation to change now.

The late author Erma Bombeck chalked this up as the inherent difference between men and women, citing her husband's aversion to nailing holes in the wall. His excuses ranged from the expiration of a calendar in twelve months to baby pictures that became obsolete as the children grew. On the other hand, she preferred the *"necessities of life"* covering every white space in their house. I think our husbands may be related.

And then there's parenting. The actor/comedian Ray Romano explains it like this: "Having children is like living in a frat house:

11

nobody sleeps, everything's broken, and there's a lot of throwing up." Whether they are two, twelve, or twenty, children exasperate us when they refuse to adhere to our well-oiled plans for their lives. Frustration is especially prevalent with a child who suffers from substance abuse. Going through the recovery process of addiction with a child is akin to riding a roller coaster. At the top of the ride, your child is working the program, taking the steps, and making great strides in changing his life. But relapse creates the same freefall sensation as the roller coaster plunge. You can do nothing to stop it. Your stomach turns. You may even throw up. But most overwhelming is the feeling of frustration. When you thought eternal recovery was imminent comes the reminder that you are still riding the rails of relapse.

David knew frustration well. God chose him to rule as king of Israel, but a jealous King Saul tormented him for years, trying to kill him. David ran from Saul, hiding in caves and surviving on whatever those loyal to him could provide. Opportunities arose many times for David to kill Saul, but he chose not to because he bore a loving and forgiving heart. (1 Samuel 18-24)

David often cried out in frustration to the Lord for mercy. He struggled with his faith, but in every one of the seventy-five psalms written or attributed to David, he concludes by praising God and giving Him glory.

As the late, great comedian Gilda Radner's character Roseanne Roseannadanna used to proclaim, "It's always something." Life is a crapshoot, and we wake up each morning to another roll of the die. Whether we discover a lump in our breast or win the lottery, the frustration of uncertainty weighs heavily. If we take a page from David's playbook, asking God for a countenance of peace instead of giving voice to our irritations, we can enjoy our days frustration-free. We can take comfort in Matthew 11:28-29: "Come to me, all you who are weary and burdened, and I will give you rest. Take my yoke upon you and learn from me, for I am gentle and humble in heart, and you will find rest for your souls."

And maybe those pesky nail holes of life will cease to frustrate you.

UNCERTAINTY
Fear Not the Evil of Uncertainty

"'I wish I could be like people.' Just then a fly flew by.
The chameleon was very hungry. But the chameleon was very mixed up.
It was a little of this and it was a little of that. And it couldn't catch the
fly."

The Mixed-Up Chameleon by Eric Carle

A chameleon aspires to be like other animals but can't decide which one. His aspirations include being "handsome like a flamingo, smart like a fox, and funny like a seal." When his new patchwork body, comprised of many animal parts, prevents him from catching a fly as he once could, he realizes that his original design was perfect for him.

The chameleon's indecision reminds me of this quote: "In these times, I don't, in a manner of speaking, know what I want; perhaps I don't want what I know and want what I don't know." (Marsilio Ficino). What?? It is a head-scratcher, but it speaks to our need to be or have something different than what we are or possess. What that may be is undefinable, but we know it will be better. Like in the case of the chameleon, this ambivalence often leaves us even more unfulfilled.

If there was ever a season of uncertainty, it is that of motherhood. We tread lightly and thoughtfully through every decision, hoping to land softly and without mishap. Other times, we throw caution to the wind and hope for the best. Sometimes, we win, and sometimes we lose, no matter which strategy we use.

My twins were born at twenty-seven weeks. When I went into premature labor and was mandated bed rest, I was confident that if I just lay perfectly still, I would carry them to full term. That self-assurance dissipated with each labor pain, and despite the doctors' best efforts to stave off delivery, my tiny two-pound babies came into this world. They were quickly whisked away and enveloped in saran wrap to preserve every ounce of body heat until they could be placed into lifesaving incubators. For two and a half months, I alternated between caring for my husband and two-and-a-half-year-old son at home and sitting bedside with two extremely sick infants. Terms like "low saturation rates" and "bradycardia" became my new lexicon. Late-night calls from NICU nurses that one of them had taken a turn for the worse

13

necessitated a return to the hospital. Uncertainty became my middle name.

Once my babies were healthy enough to go home, our family of five settled into a quasi-normal life, albeit one laden with heart rate monitors, follow-up appointments, and oxygen at the ready. The doctors cautioned that there could be lingering and even life-long complications, such as "retinopathy of prematurity" (eye disease), respiratory distress/apnea (babies born too early often "forget" to breathe), auditory processing difficulties, and hearing loss. Once, after settling Patrick in the car, I slammed the door and became alarmed by his lack of a startle reflex. I immediately became hyper focused on the future with a deaf child. His little ears were still maturing, but the uncertainty drove me to a place I did not need to go.

The U-word paid us another unwelcome visit on their first Christmas. As I bustled about the house that Christmas Eve, simultaneously preparing for the holiday while caring for two fragile babies and one very Santa-obsessed little boy, Patrick's heart monitor alarm began chirping. Assuming his wires needed adjustment, I quickly dismissed that diagnosis when I saw Patrick's lips had taken on a slightly blue tinge. This was by no means a false alarm. I summoned my husband home, loaded everybody in the car, and raced to the pediatrician's office in downtown Charleston. I don't know how many times that alarm went off as we crossed over the Cooper River, but I knew that stimulating his breathing was a matter of life or death. When they transported my extremely sick baby by ambulance a mere two blocks to the hospital, I realized the situation was dire.

Christmas that year was less than festive. The joy of watching my son discover that Santa had delivered (and I still don't remember how we pulled that off) fell under a pall of paralyzing fear that his brother was fighting for his life, felled by RSV. Nori was not to be outdone and succumbed to this disease the day following Christmas. It was not a Hallmark card, "send your very best" kind of year.

Few stories in the Bible divine the course of uncertainty to success more than that of Moses. That God appeared to him in the form of a burning bush to command that Moses lead the Israelites out of Egypt would cause anyone to doubt the validity of that confrontation. But Moses' willingness to do as God asked is a testament to the power of faith and resilience over doubt and uncertainty.

14

Psalm 23 reminds us, "Even though I walk through the darkest valley, I will fear no evil, for you are with me; your rod and your staff, they comfort me." My two tiny preemies are now adults. They suffer no limitations from their precarious beginnings, but they have dealt with life-altering illnesses in recent years. But the God who saved them all those years ago continues to watch over them. I have walked through the darkest valleys of uncertainty and fear, but His light of hope continues to burn bright. It will never dim if I fuel the flame with unwavering trust.

The "Teeny Preemies" Patrick and Nori

DISHONESTY
Wearing Masks of Deceit

"I admire Ping's great courage to appear before me with the empty truth, and now I reward him with my entire kingdom and make him Emperor of all the land."

The Empty Pot by Demi

Set in China, an aging Emperor announces that he will soon need to name a successor to rule the kingdom and tend to his flower garden. He gives each child in the kingdom one seed and declares that whoever grows the best flower will succeed him. When the day of the competition arrives, Ping is the only one unable to get his seed to grow. All the other children bring in lush plants, but Ping can only present an empty pot. The emperor is pleased with Ping because he is the only child who came forth with the original seed. He had given all the children cooked seeds, and when they would not grow, everyone but Ping replaced them with seeds that would flourish. The emperor declares Ping the winner and declares him his successor. He rewards Ping for his honesty.

Mark Twain once said, "If you tell the truth, you don't have to remember anything."

Children abide by this admonition with ease. Brutally unfiltered, they don't hesitate to call a spade a spade—or fat, ugly, smelly, etc. Become a kindergarten teacher if you want to be privy to a family's dirty little secrets. I will take to my grave comments students shared with me that their parents would pay good money not to be aired for public consumption.

As children grow, they realize that fabricating tales or blaming others deflects self-incrimination. It begins innocently enough, like "the dog ate my homework." But lying is a slippery slope, and when the tangled webs of deceit are woven with sneaking, half-truths, or evidence tampering, the lines of truth and untruth blur to the point of extinction. Hidden behind masks of deceit that impair moral vision, distinguishing fact from fiction is comparable to scrutinizing our reflections in a funhouse mirror. The truth becomes a warped, distorted version of reality.

In the Bible, Rebekah helped her son Jacob perform a very deceptive (albeit creative) lie. By order of birth, Esau was to become the family's leader, but he gave those rights to Jacob in exchange for food when he came home hungry one day after working in the fields. When their father, Issac, became terminal, Rebekah prepared a feast during which Isaac would formally pass on his birthright to Esau, unaware that Jacob now had ownership. Rebekah felt Jacob deserved it more, so she devised a plan to disguise Jacob as Esau. Because Esau was hirsute and Jacob was not, Rebekah applied goats' skin to Jacob's arms and clothed him with Esau's coat so that Jacob would smell like his brother. When Jacob, masquerading as Esau, served the meal to Isaac, the father fell for the ruse and granted Jacob his patrimony. Doing what we mothers do so well, Rebekah controlled the situation to her satisfaction, but her scheming caused a rift between the brothers that lasted for decades. (Genesis 27:1-40)

Since the dawn of time, mothers have woven innocent lies into the fabric of their children's lives. We've upheld the myth of Santa Claus, the Easter Bunny, and the Tooth Fairy. We've stealthily introduced veggies into their meals and pinkie promised to "watch this" every time they proudly announce a new skill. These fabrications, while harmless, do carry the bittersweet weight of our children's growing independence when they no longer believe our nonsense.

When our children exhibit deceitful behaviors, especially those damaging to themselves or others, we react by dismissing, ignoring, or denying this conduct. We no longer want to "watch this"; instead, we look the other way. Betrayals of Boogieman proportions replace the innocent, fictional fibs of Santa and Company.

As mothers, we, like Rebekah, love to manipulate circumstances in favor of our children. We masquerade as traffic controllers, diverting the truth about our children's behaviors from public consumption. But sweeping their problems under rugs is akin to hiding veggies in their food, magnified by a thousand. They will eventually taste the consequences of their behaviors, despite our best efforts to render them undigestible. Anyway, in this instant-feed world, one would be hard-pressed to find a rug under which to hide their issues. I am fortunate to have friends who speak the language of truth about their children's imperfections and embrace each other with acceptance and love. The ability to speak honestly without judgment has been life-changing for me.

John 8:32 reminds us that if we speak the truth, it will set us free. The Chinese children who substituted their seeds were denied the privilege of taking over the kingdom and held captive by their deception. Ping's empty pot, teeming with honesty, was favored by the emperor over those blooms of betrayal. In the insightful words of Amanda Richardson, "In a world where everyone wears a mask, it's a privilege to see a soul."

Halloween 1998

A Cure for the Chicken Little Syndrome

"Supposing a tree fell down, Pooh, when we were underneath it?"
"Supposing it didn't," said Pooh.
After careful thought, Piglet was comforted by this.

Winnie the Pooh by A. A. Milne

      In 2000, the Canadian Medical Association Journal published a tongue-in-cheek article that suggested the characters of this classic children's book all suffered from mental illness. Pooh's obsession with honey indicates an eating disorder, Eeyore's bleak outlook on life suggests depression, and Rabbit's orderly and obsessive care of his garden evokes signs of OCD. Perpetually bouncing Tigger exhibits the benchmarks of ADHD, while Owl's belief that he is wiser than everyone else demonstrates narcissism. In perpetual worry, Piglet's favorite phrase, *"Oh, dear,"* implies a generalized anxiety disorder. All the animals feed off Christopher's changing moods, indicative of schizophrenia.[5]

      Of these characters, I identify most with Piglet. I suffer from Chicken Little syndrome when it comes to my children's mental, physical, and emotional health. It does not matter how picture-perfect the sky is; it will eventually fall. Max Lucado says, *"It's not so much a storm as the certainty that one is coming. Always…coming. Sunny days are just an interlude."* [6] We often associate anxiety with fear, but they are "cousins, not twins." As Lucado explains, fear *sees* a threat. Anxiety *imagines* one. I am fearful that something will happen to my children, but my anxiety conjures up images of the monster that will devour them.

      According to Forbes Health, about 31% of adults will suffer from an anxiety disorder at some time in their lives.[7] Another article explains that our brains are wired for safety and function, much like a

---

[5] Shea, Sarah E. "Pathology in the Hundred Acre Wood: A Neurodevelopmental Perspective on A.A. Milne." *National Library of Medicine,* 12 December 2000.

[6] Lucado, Max. *Anxious for Nothing: Finding Calm in a Chaotic World.* Nashville, TN: Thomas Nelson, 2017.

[7] Booth, Jessica. "Anxiety Statistics and Facts." *Forbes Health,* 13 October 2023.

flow chart. Lived experiences allow us to answer "yes" when faced with familiar scenarios to draw upon. The unknowns require more energy, thus exacerbating our anxiety levels.[8]

When my youngest son was in the fifth grade, he began calling me at the end of the day to make sure I was coming to get him. I had been taking and picking him up from school every day since kindergarten, so I was puzzled about why he needed reassurance. Except for a handful of times caused by circumstances beyond my control, I prided myself on punctuality. It made no sense. Years later, my mom's "coulda-shoulda-woulda" brain made the correlation between his behavior and an anxiety disorder. If my mom's telepathy had sensed this disorder earlier then, would it have spared him the repercussions of it later in life? My brain wants to take the blame, but my heart knows better.

Anxiety also affected my brother with devastating consequences. At the age of fifteen, I welcomed a second brother. He was unplanned, but his addition to our family brought us unimaginable joy. Brock committed suicide at the age of forty-two when the ravages of anxiety and bipolar disease became unbearable. I still carry tremendous guilt that I did not do more to help him. But at the time, commitments to my husband, children, and work left little energy to deal with his problems. I regret my impatient desire for him to "snap out of it." After facing mental health struggles myself, as well as with my children, I know now that this was not an option for him. But through growth and maturity in my faith, I recognize my inculpability and realize that this was, as hard as it is to understand, part of God's plan.

Anxiety was prevalent even in biblical times. Jehoshaphat was the fourth ruler of Judah and one of the most successful. He struggled with anxiety when making decisions on behalf of his people, but he always went to God in prayer. When an enormous contingent of his enemies threatened to attack, God assured him that the battle would be won, and it was. His trust in God assuaged his anxiety. (2 Chronicles 20:1-19)

Anxiety is a thief of time and a pilferer of peace. The longer we fret about the future and lament the past, the more we miss opportunities to embrace the goodness of today. This quote embraces the futility of anxiety: "I have to remind myself all the time that being

---

[8] Plum, Karen. "Unlocking Psychological Safety." *Advanced Workplace Associates,* 6 July 2020.

afraid of things going wrong isn't the way to make things go right."
(Unknown)

   We can follow Jehosophat's example when faced with stressful
decisions and heed the promise of Philippians 4:6-7: "Do not be
anxious about anything, but in everything, through prayer and petition
with thanksgiving, let your requests be made known to God. And the
peace of God, which surpasses understanding, will guard your hearts
and minds in Christ Jesus."

   And if the sky does fall, God's umbrella of protection will shield
us from the deluge.

"Petey Playing in the Rain"
1996

GUILT
Guilty Gertie

"I'd rather feel silly, excited, or glad,
Than cranky or grumpy, discouraged, or sad.
But moods are just something that happen each day.
Whatever I'm feeling inside is okay."

Today I Feel Silly and Other Moods that Make My Day by Jamie Lee
Curtis (author) and Laura Cornell (illustrator)

A comforting book for children, Jamie Lee Curtis addresses all
the emotions that children encounter. She reassures her young readers
that ALL feelings…grumpy, silly, angry, confused, happy, or sad…are
valid.

This book was a perennial favorite of mine while teaching
kindergarten. Written for young children, it also pairs well with the
seasons of motherhood. I dare you to name one mother who has not
fielded this gamut of emotions while raising children. Curtis does not,
however, address the emotion that most often rocks us to our core:
Guilt.

If you are a mother, guilt can wreak havoc on your confidence.
It is your constant companion while navigating relationships with your
children. This voice of doubt lurks behind every decision you make
about your child's future. It is the specter of hindsight that haunts you,
the nights you lie awake wondering how you could have prevented the
illness, the failure, or the hurt.

Before succumbing to the lure of that insidious rabbit hole,
consider embracing the *"Three C's"* motto of my mother's support
group: "I didn't cause it, I can't control it, and I can't cure it." No
matter how often you drag your children to church or the woodshed,
free will can hijack them despite every parenting hack known to man.
"Come to Jesus meetings" only work if Jesus himself attends. And even
that strategy is questionable.

Guilt trips are the bane of a mother's existence. And the crazy
train is how we usually travel. We can thank Adam and Eve, the first
parents, for establishing a pattern that continues today. We cover up,
play the blame game, and try to rationalize our actions to make us feel
better. But that tiny bite of an apple binds us forever to guilt and shame.

Speaking of guilt, we just got a new puppy. I know what you are thinking: "What were you thinking?" Our newest troublemaker is Gertie, a miniature dachshund weighing eight pounds soaking wet. Her petite frame contradicts her life-size personality, especially when avoiding commands, hence her nickname, Obstinate Daughter. Her puppy dog eyes proclaim righteous innocence, but incriminating evidence convicts her every single time.

We crate-trained Gertie, an essential practice for puppies. Her initial whining and whimpering were a small price to pay to avoid the cost of future chaos. Eventually, Gertie looked forward to kennel time and the comfort and safety of her home.

Crate training is not unlike raising children. Puppies need the boundaries and structure that crates provide; children do too. Not a crate, mind you (although that has crossed my mind), but the symbolic enclosure of conformity. And this requires parents to adhere firmly to their rules and regulations. (I am not good at taking my own advice. Gertie now sleeps in our bed.) Children can be master manipulators, and their weapon of choice is guilt. They can "so and so's mother lets them" till the cows come home, and we must be prepared to stand our ground.

But eventually, they graduate from the confines of their "cages" into a world where rules are fast and loose. We can only hope that the years of structure are ingrained so deeply that the lure of bad choices does not tempt them beyond what they can withstand. When we do find ourselves in a situation with a child who has tipped a toe in the river of emancipation with questionable results, we default to self-blame and false guilt. Colin Smith explains it this way: "False guilt comes when we take responsibility for something that was not our calling or is not under our control." On the contrary, "True guilt comes when we shirk responsibility for something that is the call or command of God." Smith adds, "The answer to false guilt is truth. The answer to true guilt is grace."[9] We have been given the grace of forgiveness through Jesus Christ for our transgressions, as assured in Proverbs 28:13: "Whoever conceals their sins does not prosper, but the one who confesses and renounces them finds mercy."

As mothers, we must deny ourselves the burden of

---

[9] Smith, Colin. *Understand Your Guilt: Its Causes and Answers.* Retrieved from *Open the Bible with Pastor Colin.* 18 November 2018.

false guilt, taking the blame for our children's poor decisions, because God provides the grace of forgiveness for their actions. We become emancipated from the burden of guilt when we shed the shackles of self-incrimination.

If you still fancy a guilt trip, get a puppy.

GUILTY GERTIE

Control and the Red Sweater Vest

"Mean Jean was Recess Queen and nobody said anything different. Nobody swung until Mean Jean swung. Nobody kicked until Mean Jean kicked. Nobody bounced until Mean Jean bounced."

The Recess Queen by Alexis O'Neill

Mean Jean is a playground bully. Control is her superpower until a new student teaches her that kindness is a better method of gaining acceptance. If you are a mother and enjoy dictating every aspect of your child's life, you might feel a certain kinship to Mean Jean.

We are heading back into two of my favorite times of the year: back-to-school and college football season. Scrolling through those social media posts of kids dressed in their new clothes and carrying spotless backpacks and lunchboxes filled with freshly sharpened pencils and nutritious lunches makes me happy. Even happier are the mothers who packed them. I have warm memories of those days, but others are cringe-worthy because of my fondness for control.

In her book, *It's All Under Control,* Jennifer Dukes Lee asserts that today's parents are "a society of problem solvers and outcome managers." Instead of being helicopter parents "hovering over our kids' lives," we have become "lawnmower parents," clearing the path for our children so that they do not fail."[10]

While raising my three children, I won Lawnmower of the Year several times. Not wanting a child to fail an assignment, I completed it. Lost phone? Here's a new one. And heaven forbid they got hungry when that lunchbox failed to make it out of the car! In retrospect, I should have let them fail and go without. If I let them suffer some consequences, they may have learned valuable life lessons from these reality checks.

Perhaps my favorite Mommy Manipulation Move occurred when my oldest son interviewed for a coveted spot at Charleston School of the Arts. This magnet school accepts the district's most talented artists, musicians, dancers, and writers. Pete applied as a visual arts major, and his portfolio was jaw-dropping. The art was one

---

[10] Lee, Jennifer Dukes. *It's All Under Control: A Journey of Letting Go, Hanging On, and Finding Peace You Almost Forgot Was Possible.* Carol Stream, IL: Tyndale House Publishing, 2018.

hundred percent his, but I may have helped a little with the presentation. Well, maybe a lot. To ensure a seamless first impression, I also bought him a red sweater vest and khaki pants so that he would not present the typical teenage grungy, I-don't-give-a-rat's-tail image.

I got lost en route to the interview because I was not in line when God was handing out directional capabilities. I called my husband, crying hysterically that we would not make it and that I had ruined my child's life. We arrived just in the nick of time, with Pete's life wholly intact. I could not have been prouder of my boy, all decked out in his frat brother ensemble, toting his award-worthy portfolio. Until I realized he stood out like a sore thumb amidst the sea of kids clad in the typical uniform of t-shirt, shorts, and flipflops. To this day, I am thankful his peers did not beat him up in the parking lot.

Control and manipulation have been around since God created humans. The serpent convinced Eve to eat the forbidden fruit, promising she would not die. Furthermore, if she ate the fruit, her "eyes would be opened," and she would "be like God, knowing good and evil." (Genesis 3:5). She even used her feminine wiles to convince poor Adam to do the same, leaving them naked and ashamed, and hiding from God.

Mothers often approach parenting with serpent-like deception. We bribe, bargain, and threaten to get our children to conform to our wishes. When our children are young, we administer "time outs" and revoke privileges. Later, we add curfews and conditions to our arsenal. These methods may prove effective during the early and formative years, but we lose our parenting leverage during the emancipated teen and early adult era. We can Life360 them to death, but no tracking app in existence can divert them from poor decision-making.

It is hard. We do not want our children to suffer or do without. We try to change but revert to our old selves. Lee sums it up: "Here's what my regression looked like: I again became a self-reliant woman who would go to Google before God, who would try to manage outcomes."

It is easy to rely on Google for answers. We can self-diagnose health issues, acquire advice to fix our devices and keep abreast of impending natural disasters in real time. However, Google is not privy to our situations and can only provide one-size-fits-all solutions. Prayer is the only source of tailored resolutions.

Dictionary.com defines control as "the power to influence or direct people's behavior or the course of events," implying a mechanical and powerful means of persuasion. But the Bible refutes these depictions of power. It redefines power *"as a by-product of gentleness, sacrifice, and even suffering."*[11] As humans, our only means of control is faith. As Pastor Joel Schmidgall states, "You can have faith, or you can have control, but you cannot have both."

Jean Wise uses the trapeze act, The Flying Rodleighs, as an analogy between faith and control. Flying unencumbered negates the flyer's control and places it entirely in the catcher's possession. The flyer must stretch out his arms and believe he will be caught. The flyer or the catcher could face injury if the flyer grabs onto the catcher's wrists.[12] We can liken this to our roles as mothers. Having faith allows us to let go and relinquish control to God.

The Serenity Prayer addresses control this way: "God, grant me the serenity to accept the things I cannot change, the courage to change the things I can, and the wisdom to know the difference." Only when we adopt the free-flying faith of the trapeze artists will we find the serenity that God offers. As we are reminded in Proverbs 19:21, "Many are the plans in the mind of a man, but it is the purpose of the Lord that will stand."

"The Red Sweater Vest"

[11] Grieg, Pete. *God on Mute: Engaging the Silence of Unanswered Prayers.* Ada, MI: Baker Publishing Group, 2007.

[12] Wise, Jean. "Henri Nouwen's Story About the Flyer and the Catcher ." *Healthy Spirituality*, 31 October 2013.

Perfection in the Plough Mud

"I'm no good at this. I QUIT."

The Most Magnificent Thing by Ashley Spires

A little girl decides she will make the most magnificent thing but soon realizes that making that magnificent thing takes more work. After repeated attempts fail, she gets so mad that she quits. Her canine "assistant" convinces her to go for a walk, and "bit by bit, the mad gets pushed out of her head." She returns to the project with a renewed attitude and completes it. The finished project may not have aligned with her original plans, but eliminating the idol of perfection enabled her to accept the constraints of her abilities. "Have no fear of perfection – you'll never reach it." Salvador Dali was spot on with this nugget of wisdom. As a perfectionistic control freak, I could have benefited from that advice when I assumed I had the power to create a perfect life, complete with perfect children.

Apparently, those perfectionist tendencies had yet to develop during my teenage years. Mom loved to tell the story about calling 911, fearing our home had been broken into, and the responders questioned whether my room had been ransacked. No, it had not, Mr. 911 Smarty-Pants Responders. It was my acquired taste at the time, thank you very much.

My firstborn got married last September. In three days, our home was the setting for three events. For months, I toiled tirelessly to ensure the weekend went off without a hitch. The memory of whipping up mini banana puddings in a three-a.m. sleep-deprived fog is seared into my brain.

Then there was the plough mud incident. While scavenging for driftwood to use on the wedding arch, I found myself mired waist-deep in this coastal quicksand. Listen carefully when I tell you this: Do not, under any circumstances, wear flip-flops while scavenging for driftwood in plough mud. You may surface, but your flip-flops will not. They will be lost to the ages along with Jimmy Buffett's shaker of salt. The burning question here is how I found myself in said situation. Obviously, my brain was not firing on all cylinders. But I will also pass on this tidbit: Removing dried plough mud from your body (floor mats, steering wheel, and seat) requires more than the simple squirt of a garden hose. You haven't lived until you've bathed yourself under the PSI pressure of a car wash nozzle. I do not doubt that my muddy, barefoot legacy is preserved in security camera eternity.

But I digress. The weekend turned out beautifully, but not without some drama. We played many fun games, like "Find the Missing Bridesmaid" and "Quick Remedies for a Kick in the Crotch". But as the processional music began, it was as if drama took a bow and perfection graced center stage. Those dirty little secrets never made the wedding album cut.

Seeking perfection is a form of idolatry, and God has made it perfectly clear how he feels about that. Number one on His List of Ten Things Not to Do cautions us to "not have other gods before me." (Exodus 20:3). This includes our children.

I confess to breaking this commandment many times throughout my children's lives. Using my well-honed ability to manipulate and control, I paved a College-Career-Couple-Children path, after which we would all live happily ever after. As the saying goes, we plan, and God laughs.

In her book *Breaking Up with Perfect,* Amy Carroll reminds us that perfection "is a work we try to do ourselves." In reality, it is "a work that God accomplishes...as we surrender our lists and all of ourselves to Him".[13] I sacrificed a lot of sleep, weight, energy, and time on the altar of perfection when I refused to allow His plans to take precedence over mine.

The high bar we set for our children is only exacerbated by social media. The trend of seeking advice from "influencers" to assimilate with societal standards promotes the quest for perfection. Instead of focusing on individual potential and authenticity, identifying with sameness is preferred, catapulting them into social schizophrenia. To quote Judy Garland, pursuing "second-rate versions" of other people is more enticing than "first-rate versions" of themselves. This Stepford Wife mentality prevents us from being "the people that make meaning, not the thing that is made." [14]

If we genuinely seek perfection, we must seek the influence of scripture, not influencers' sway. Facebook and Faith cannot coexist. It is only when we smash society's idols and embrace God's sovereign

---

[13] Carroll, Amy. *Breaking Up with Perfect.* Brentwood, TN: Howard Books, 2015.
[14] *Barbie.* Dir. Greta Gerwig, 2023.

shrine that we will be "perfect as our Father is perfect" (Matthew 5:48). Not plastic Barbie perfect, but whole and complete.

If you are navigating life with a child who has cancer, mental illness, substance abuse disorder, the challenges of an extra chromosome or is incarcerated, hold close the promise of Jeremiah 29:11. He will protect that child from harm and grant him "hope and a future." I found that hope when I allowed myself to emerge from the plough mud of my perfection and humbled myself before Him in acceptance of my Real-World Life.

The wedding weekend was memorable, but not without some hiccups. That the D.J. forgot to include an essential song in his playlist or that we had to abandon our sparkler send-off due to an outgoing tide, forcing us to disembark at a neighbor's dock, did little to diminish the sanctity of the celebration. Not one attendee will remember these mishaps (or were even aware of them), but they will hold close the moment Pete and Elena vowed to love and cherish each other, surrounded by friends, family, the sparkling waters of the ocean, and a blue sky that was heaven sent. As for me, I exchanged plough mud and banana pudding perfection for the flawlessness of a day that only God can provide.

By the way, the arch was built thanks to Pete's brother, Patrick, and no plough mud was sacrificed in its making.

The Danger of Anger

"She kicks, she screams. She wants to smash the world to smithereens."

When Sophie Gets Really, Really Angry by Molly Bang

When her mom tells her to give her sister a turn with the toy gorilla, Sophie does not listen. She is like a "volcano ready to explode." Eventually, she learns that running in the woods calms her anger, allowing her to return home relaxed and collected.

Hell hath no fury like a child who doesn't get her way. Some people's indignation follows them throughout their lives. My husband seems to think I may be one of them.

At a recent Masters Golf Tournament in Augusta, Georgia, the weather was atrociously inclement, and three trees fell from the high winds. In addition to the weather, chances to command the lead fell short due to wayward drives off the tee and putts gone awry. But golf is a gentleman's sport, and apparently, "hissy fits" (Southernism for childish temper tantrums) are frowned upon. My husband snorted when I made the comment that golfing would seriously challenge my Southern refinement. He has personally witnessed some of my greatest attempts at sanctimonious retaliation. A golf club in my hot-headed hands would not end well.

When my first son was born, Pete and I took him to downtown Charleston to stroll and grab a bite to eat. It was a sunny day, with the windows of many restaurants open. rePete began crying at one point as we passed two ladies lunching. They loudly commented, "That baby needs to get out of the sun." As a brand spanking new mom, I lost all hormonal control and proceeded to tell them where THEY could "get." Not my most stellar parenting moment.

Since COVID's invasion and subsequent disruption of our lives, the anger factor in this nation has grown exponentially. Coping mechanisms for navigating this new normal are often divisive and polarizing. Given the inability to air grievances face to face, we have taken to online messaging and social media rants. Our confrontations are rude and hateful, given the protection from physical retribution and the mask of anonymity. Rage is no longer confined to the road. We now see it on airplanes, grocery stores, offices, and parking lots. We are a nation of overgrown toddlers throwing tantrums.

In his book *Going to Pieces Without Falling Apart*, Dr. Mark Epstein surmises that the root of anger is often fear. He cites fear as *"just another response to what we cannot control. And anger is an attempt to override fear."*[15] Anger is a valid emotional response to perceived danger, but it can be catastrophic when it spirals out of control. In the words of Eleanor Roosevelt, "Anger is one letter short of danger."

The Bible attempts to put a time limit on anger. In Ephesians 4:26-27 we are advised, "In your anger do not sin: Do not let the sun go down while you are still angry, and do not give the devil a foothold.*"*

Anger is like a watched pot that never boils. It simmers and festers, bubbles of rage submerged beneath the surface. If we take our eyes off the pot and allow those bubbles to erupt and spill over, we find ourselves in regrettable situations requiring damage control. What consumes our minds eventually makes it out of our mouths, and there is no putting the genie back in the bottle. Ambrose Bierce once said, "Speak when you are angry, and you will make the best speech you will ever regret."

If I have learned one thing as a mother, it is that anger has never solved one single conflict with my children. I regret every time I failed to abide by the advice to "say it like you mean it, but don't say it mean." A Chinese proverb speaks to this anguish: *"If you are patient in one moment of anger, you will escape a hundred days of sorrow."*

That is good advice for a gal prone to hissy fits.

---

[15] Epstein, Mark M.D... *Going to Pieces Without Falling Apart.* New York City: Penguin Random House, 1999.

PAIN AND SUFFERING
Pruning the Pain and Suffering

"And then came the winter...the snow and the sleet! And icicles hung from his trunk and his feet. But Horton kept sitting, and said with a sneeze,
"I'll stay on this egg and won't let it freeze.
I meant what I said and I said what I meant...
An elephant's faithful, one hundred percent!"

Horton Hatches the Egg by Dr Seuss

When lazy bird Mayzie convinces Horton to sit on her egg while she vacations, he does not realize Mayzie has no plans to return. But Horton remains loyal to his promise of "one hundred percent" and sits on the egg through seasonal changes, ridicule from friends, and the threat of theft. When Mayzie tries to reclaim the egg 51 weeks later, with Horton still faithfully compliant to his vow, the egg hatches, and a small elephant with wings emerges.

Horton faces the erratic challenges of nature's four seasons in the same way mothers cycle through the seasons of motherhood. Whether changing diapers, chauffeuring, chaperoning, or choosing colleges, each stage presents unique stressors. A baby bird abandons the comfort of its nest as soon as it can fly, while our children emerge from the womb but remain forever tethered to us by our heartstrings. Contrary to popular opinion, the "empty nest" is an urban legend.

It is a blessing and an honor that three people call me "mom," but that title was hard-earned. Infertility and prematurity almost defied their very existence. Their grown-up problems threatened to "rock me like a hurricane." (The Scorpions, 1984) However, even those setbacks are in no way comparable to the ones Job experienced.

Once wealthy in both finances and family, Job suffered the loss of his ten children, his flocks and herds, his servants, his house, and his wife's confidence. In addition, his body bore the ravages of painful boils, rendering him unrecognizable to his friends. Job's lamentations to God were frequent and accusatory, punctuated by cries for understanding. But, never, not once, did he cease praying to God for deliverance. While He never divulged a reason for allowing such pain, God did reassure Job of His existence and sat with him in the silence of his suffering. (Job 1:1-10)

To shed an academic understanding of why a loving God might allow pain and suffering, British novelist Pico Iyer asserts that suffering brings clarity and illumination. In Eastern societies, suffering is the "first rule of life." They believe that "calamity cracks you open, moves you to change your ways."[16] C. S. Lewis clarifies it like this: "God whispers to us in our pleasures, speaks in our conscience, but shouts in our pain: it is His megaphone to rouse a deaf world."[17] He wants us to awaken to His surroundings outside of our self-absorption and glorify Him.

When motherhood gets messy, it helps me to reflect on Pete Grieg's analogy of suffering to that of the olive tree. In his book, *God on Mute: Engaging the Silence of Unanswered Prayers*, Grieg explains that olive oil was a valuable resource of the ancient world and that the only way to extract it from the olive was to crush it to a pulp. He compares this to suffering in our lives. The intense pressure and destruction of something good are often exchanged for something better.[18] As Elisabeth Elliott, a missionary whose first husband died at the hands of Ecuadoran tribe members, points out, "There are a good many things in this life that we really can't do anything about, but that God wants us to do something with."

Sarah Ban Breathnach likens this to pruning a plant. While it does not make sense to cut back on something thriving, plants require this for healthy growth. Similarly, life accidents prune us back, and pain provides the necessary catalyst for our maturation. "Our souls become broken fields, plowed by pain."[19]

When we witness pain and suffering in our children's lives, we must remember that God wants to do something with it. And that is something that complacency and contentment can never teach.

---

[16] Iyer, Pico." The Value of Suffering." *The New York Times,* 7 September 2013.

[17] Lewis, C. S. *The Problem of Pain.* San Francisco: Harper One, 2015.

[18] Grieg, Pete. *God on Mute: Engaging the Silence of Unanswered Prayer.* Ada, MI: Baker Publishing, 2011.

[19] Breathnah, Sarah Ban. *Simple Abundance: A Daybook of Comfort and Joy.* New York City: Grand Central Publishing, 2009.

Facing Fear with Faith

"'Child, come out from under that bed. It's only thunder you're hearing,' my grandma said."

Thunder Cake by Patricia Polacco

When a loud clap of thunder booms, Grandma announces that it is Thunder Cake baking weather, a ruse to assuage her granddaughter's fears. Because a real Thunder Cake must reach the oven before the storm arrives, the urgency to gather and assemble the ingredients replaces the anxiety of the pending storm with the anticipation of savoring the dessert. Grandma is passing on the Thunder Cake baking strategy her Babushka used to help her overcome her fear of thunder.

Fear assails us at every stage of life. Young children are afraid of the dark. The idea of not fitting in terrifies teenagers. Not finding a life partner haunts young adults. Seniors dread the loss of independence. And the fear of dying is a natural and unavoidable concern for everyone except my mother.

My mom passed away on June 5, 2021. Up until her Myelodysplastic Syndrome diagnosis, I barely remember her being sick. In 80 years, she went to the hospital three times, all to give birth. The doctors managed her disease for two years, and I had begun to believe that she would survive. She fought valiantly, but her treatment options eventually dwindled. Walking out of the doctor's office after essentially being handed a death sentence, she commented, "Well, I didn't expect that."

There was an occurrence a few days before she died that seemed to portend her heavenly transition. A visitor to the house asked Mom to sit on Dad's lap to take a picture. High school sweethearts and married for 62 years that lap-sitting ship sailed years ago. She complied, and the image was taken. The result was both chilling and peaceful. In the photo, Mom appears to be enveloped by an aura, angelic in her composure. I had more questions than answers, but her calm demeanor seemed to portend her imminent transition.

Daniel exhibited the same kind of fearless faith. He refused to obey after learning that King Darius had ordered his people to only pray to him and that violators would be thrown into the lion's den. In protest, he kneeled and prayed three times a day to God, sealing his fate. Expecting a bloody massacre the following morning, the den was opened to find Daniel alive and well. He credited an angel sent by God to close the lions' mouths. (Daniel 6:10-27)

As Franklin Roosevelt once said, "The only thing to fear is fear itself." Apparently, poor Eleanor was tasked with raising the children. The fears of a mother can be downright debilitating. My children and I recited this familiar prayer at bedtime for years: "Now I lay me down to sleep. I pray the Lord my soul to keep. If I should die before I wake, I pray the Lord my soul to take." In my opinion, this always seemed a little heavy for a child's prayer with its attempt to alleviate the fear of death. But in retrospect, given some issues we have navigated, it served as a decent insurance policy.

Many Bible passages combine fear with *not*. We are told *not* to be afraid because God has our backs, but we are also warned to fear God and to revere Him and Him alone. The dichotomy is confusing, but the Rev. Billy Graham clarified it this way: Fear is "an emotion marked by dread and concern," but it also means "awe and wonder and profound reverence."[20] How we view fear is how we define it. If we change the order of the letters *a* and *c* in *scared* to produce *sacred*, we exchange the specter of fear for unfaltering faith. As Joanna Weaver advises, instead of "conniving and striving," we begin "resting and relying." [21]

Like Grandma's ploy, when we rely on faith to make the thunder cake, we are oblivious to the storm. My mother did just that.

[20] BGEA Admin. "Answers." *Billy Graham Evangelical Association,* 14 October 2020.

[21] Weaver, Joanna. *Embracing Trust.* Grand Rapid, MI: Revell Books, 2022.

Parenting PTSD

"Nothing can change the terrible thing that Sherman saw, but now he does not feel so mean. He is not so scared or worried. His stomach does not hurt as much. And the bad dreams hardly ever happen."

A Terrible Thing Happened by Sasha J. Mudlaff (author) and Cary Pillo (illustrator)

Sherman witnesses something terrible that causes him to have stomach aches, bad dreams, and angry feelings. However, Ms. Maple is a grown-up who understands Sherman, and through talking and drawing, she gets Sherman to share his feelings. As a result, the physical manifestations of his trauma no longer haunt him.

According to the American Psychiatric Association, "posttraumatic stress disorder" (PTSD) is a psychiatric disorder that "can occur in people who have experienced or witnessed a traumatic event, series of events, or set of circumstances." In addition, PTSD and substance abuse are often co-occurring. People seeking treatment for PTSD are 14 times more likely to be diagnosed with SUD.[22]   While we most associate PTSD with members of the military who have witnessed atrocities in combat, PTSD can also affect parents who have navigated life-changing experiences with their children.

I love being a mother, but I did spend a little time in parenting purgatory. As of this writing, my children are doing well.
But unlike a computer, my hard drive cannot be erased and reset. Traumatic events stick like barnacles to the bottom of a boat that no scraping can dislodge. A memory can trigger an immediate freefall into the pit of PTSD.

There is a scientific explanation for this. When the amygdala, the part of the brain responsible for storing emotional memory, is subjected to chronic bouts of fear, it becomes hyperactive. Mental health professionals refer to this as "amygdala hijacking," resulting in neurochemical changes. The repercussions are cognitive, emotional, and physical, including, but not limited to, rapid heart rate, heightened

[22] Posttraumatic Stress Disorder (PTSD." *American Psychiatric Association,* https://www.psychiatry.org/patients-families/ptsd.

37

blood pressure, and cardiovascular, gastrointestinal, and musculoskeletal issues.[23]

I think we can all agree that heart palpitations are a normal response when our children drive alone for the first time. Long gone are backward-facing car seats, complete with constraints that are jailbreak-worthy. We can no longer protect our children with the "original seat belt" (mom-arm-thrown-across-child's body). But as long as that driving record remains free of tickets and accidents, we lull ourselves into a semblance of peace. I'm sorry to say I was never afforded that luxury.

Research into whether male or female teenagers are better drivers tends to arrive at this consensus: Male drivers are more confident than their female counterparts, but males are more likely to engage in risky driving behaviors.[24] As a mom of two hell-on-wheels sons, I do not argue with that assertion. Now I can laugh at some of their antics, like when one son voiced incredulity that patrol officers worked in the wee hours of the morning. But another instance causes me to spiral into the abyss of PTSD.

My other son had a severe accident caused by running into the back of a semi on a busy interstate. The impact drove his right leg into his hip, causing major damage. His other leg also suffered severe injuries. At the hospital, we were told that his situation was serious and would require surgery, but his survival prognosis was good.

The next day, my husband and I went to retrieve items from his truck. While I had witnessed first-hand his physical condition at the hospital, I was not prepared for the sight of his truck. My first thought was that this was the wrong vehicle because no one could have walked away from such a devastating collision. It was mangled way beyond recognition or repair. The only explanation that he is still earthbound is that God wrapped his arms around him in such a protective embrace that his life was spared. The image of this devastation, both to the truck and to my son, will haunt me forever.

PTSD was first coined as a diagnosis in 1980, but the symptoms were recognized as early as Biblical times. Take King Saul, for example. He went to war repeatedly. He fought with spears and swords, as well as hand-to-hand combat. The extreme events he witnessed

---

[23] "Understanding Trauma in Parents of Young Addicts." *The Edge Reha,* 31 March 2017.

[24] Covington, Tara. "Men are more confident drivers, but data shows women are safer." *The Zebra.* 13 March 2024.

weighed heavily on him, distorting relationships and creating trust issues. He endured sleeplessness and night terrors and was overcome by fits of rage, all classic symptoms of PTSD. He bore permanent scars, both mentally and physically, and died a troubled soul in his final battle. (1 Samuel 9-31)

King Saul lived when no treatments were available for this affliction, but the American Psychological Association cites several modern-day intervention strategies and medications. These tactics address the physical symptoms of this disease but fail to speak to the spiritual component. An article entitled "What Would Jesus Do" fictionalizes a conversation between Jesus and a PTSD sufferer.[25] The author imagines it this way.

> *"Your trauma doesn't make Me uncomfortable.*
> *You aren't too damaged for Me to relate to.*
> *Your wound wasn't for nothing. There is purpose in your pain. The*
> *scars stay so that they can tell a story.*
> *Depend on your doctors, but abide in Me."*

1 Samuel 5:10 validates this conversation: "And the God of all grace, who called you to his eternal glory in Christ, after you have suffered a little while, will himself restore you and make you strong, firm and steadfast."

PTSD is an invisible affliction that makes it hard for others to understand. The most subtle triggers invite the sufferer down that insidious rabbit hole. We rely on physicians to manage the physical symptoms, but emotional relief remains elusive until we rely on the Great Physician for a countenance of peace. Dependence on Him negates the need for that graduate degree in PTSD.

---

[25] Owens, Jesse. "What would Jesus say to someone suffering from PTSD?" *Reboot Recovery,* 25 October 2016.

Redefining Hopelessness

"Sometimes I feel so very sad and really don't know why. Instead of playing and having fun, I cry and cry and cry."

The Way I Feel by Janan Cain

It is essential to help children identify and name their feelings. This book uses colorful images and simple verses to help children connect words to emotions. It is rare to witness hopelessness in eternally optimistic young children, but the havoc it wreaks on adults can be devastating.

Today is Father's Day and my baby brother's 47th birthday. When I was fifteen, I became a sister for the second time. This baby brother was an unplanned "slip," nicknamed "tater" by my dad's golfing buddies. If that makes no sense, understand that potatoes aren't grown from seed but from slips and sprouts rooted in mature potatoes.

Brock was a beautiful, towheaded boy, joyful from the day he was born. We spent hours on the family room floor watching him count pennies, laughing as he repeatedly exclaimed, "Can't afford it." His "sassy" (pacifier) and Raggedy Andy blanket were constant companions, and he rubbed the corner of the blanket against his face for comfort as he fell asleep. At high school football games, with my parents in the stands watching me cheer, he was passed from spectator to spectator, all waiting their turn to hold him. He was the light of our life until the ravages of mental illness extinguished that flame.

My brother is celebrating this birthday in heaven.

Brock had bipolar disorder, a mental illness that causes unusual shifts in a person's mood, energy, activity levels, and concentration. Moods range from manic to depressive episodes. He battled these demons throughout his life, occasionally finding relief, but never for long. His hopelessness manifested in numerous threats to take his life, but he never followed through. Until he did.

One of my all-time favorite movies, *Little Miss Sunshine,* is a study of hopelessness. Except for Olive, whose chubby, awkward, bespectacled self aspires to win the title in the upcoming Little Miss Sunshine beauty pageant, every member of the Hoover family suffers from some form of depression. The cast of this dark comedy consists of a gay suicidal uncle; a four-letter-loving heroin addict grandfather and Olive's pageant coach; a moody, non-communicative teenager; a mother who wears a permanent mask of stress; and an optimistically goal-obsessed, yet ironically under-achieving, father. This collectively dysfunctional family sets out in the family's ancient yellow VW van on a long-distance, mishap-filled journey to help Olive realize her dream. This journey culminates in Olive's bawdy talent performance taught to her by her grandfather before he succumbed to a drug overdose during the trip and whose body was unceremoniously toted in the back of the van. It is apparent from the opening strains of *Super Freak by* Rick James ("She's a very sexy girl that you don't bring home to mama...") that it is hardly an age-appropriate performance for a child's beauty pageant. When pageant organizers revolt against this blatant disregard for tastefulness, the family joins Olive on stage in solidarity. Olive's chances at winning this contest against a host of Little Miss Perfects were dismal. But the hopelessness of winning is overshadowed by the spark of hope that ignites this melodramatic family when circumstances bring them together.

Depression was prevalent even in Biblical times. One of the most recognized for his feelings of defeat and hopelessness was Elijah. Despite having false prophets put to death and returning the allegiance of the people of Israel to God, Queen Jezebel's threat to have him killed caused Elijah to run, overcome with fear and despair. He sat down under a solitary broom tree and prayed that he might die. "I have had enough, Lord," he said. "Take my life, for I am no better than my ancestors who have already died." (1 Kings 19:4). Like my brother, he sought relief through death, nails in his coffin of hope.

In her book *Seeing Beautiful Again*, Lysa Terkeurst relates how she wrestled with this emotion in the face of a breast cancer diagnosis. Mired in feelings of hopelessness, she struggled to feel the nearness of God. A friend reminded her that by making one simple change to the word "impossible" and placing an apostrophe between the letters I and M, impossible becomes "I'm possible." This slight change caused a massive shift in her perspective. "I'm Possible is a much more comforting way to look at anything that feels quite impossible."[26]

If asked which achievement I am most proud of, my quick and short response would be motherhood. It has also been the most

---

[26] Terkeurst, Lysa. *Seeing Beautiful Again.* Nashville, TN: Thomas Nelson, 2021.

challenging. Nothing defines hopelessness like parenting a child with struggles you can't fix. But as Jesus assured his disciples in Matthew 19:26, "…with God, all things are possible." When impossible parenting situations assault us, dependence on Him allows us to avow "I'm possible."

Despite her apparent inadequacies, Olive hoped to win the title of Little Miss Sunshine. God restored Elijah's strength so that he could continue ministering to his people, and instead of dying, Elijah was transported to heaven in a chariot of fire. Presently, my children are well and living productive lives. God made it possible. In the immortal words of Rick James, "…he will never let your spirits down."

My baby brother, Brock

Grief is Not a Gentleman

"I was very sad, too, but it helped to remember that I had told her every night, 'I'll always love you.'"

I'll Always Love You by Hans Wilhem

A little boy loves a dachshund named Elfie. Their relationship is playful until Elfie begins to age. One morning, he awakens and finds that Elfie has died during the night. He is sad but comforted that he always told Elfie he loved him.

In its traditional sense, grief is most associated with mourning a death. But not always. Sometimes, we undergo the death of a dream, the loss of a relationship, or unfulfilled hope. Especially when it relates to our children. Lysa Terkeurst refers to this grief as *"dreaming in reverse."* [27]

Regardless of origin, grief is a shapeshifter, an unplanned and unwelcome visitor. Jodie Berndt explains it this way: "Sometimes grief is a gentleman, waiting until we have time to think and feel before entering the rooms of our interior lives. Other times, grief ignores all the cues, and you weep over your salad at dinner while celebrating a friend's birthday, or tuck away into a bathroom stall at a concert and cry." [28]

We grieve because we love. There is no better example of the love/grief connection in the Bible than that of Mary's love for her only son and the grief she experienced at his death. From the time she answered the angel's call to bear God's son to the ultimate sacrifice of his death, her mother's heart beat with a confluence of emotions. Grief and love. They are impossible to separate.

In the span of three years, my family has buried my mother, my Aunt Martha (her sister), and my Uncle Buddy (Aunt Martha's husband). My brother committed suicide seven years ago, and with each additional passing, my grief feels rawer and deeper. It is certainly no gentleman. I grieve because I loved them so much.

---

[27] Terkeurst, Lysa. *Seeing Beautiful Again: 50 Devotions to Find Redemption in Every Part of Your Story.* Nashville, TN: Thomas Nelson, 2021.

[28] Berndt, Jodie. *Praying the Scriptures for Your Adult Life: 31 Days of Abiding in the Presence, Provision, and Power of God.* Grand Rapids, M: Zondervan, 2021.

Grief is a universal experience but a process as unique and organic to each person as the relationship with the deceased. There are no hard and fast rules except that there are no hard and fast rules. The five stages of grief wrap it in a pretty box and tie it neatly with a bow, but the contents are an unwelcome gift. It is tempting to hide it or hurry it, to get over it and move on, but pain that is left unattended will fester, causing physical and emotional discomfort.

Unfortunately, we live in a culture that doesn't have time for grief. In her book, *It's OK That You're Not OK: Meeting Grief and Loss in a Culture That Doesn't Understand,* the author debunks "the culturally prescribed goal of returning to a normal, 'happy' life." She asserts, "Grief is simply love in its wild and painful form. It is a natural and sane response to loss." Society seeks a remedy, a quick fix, but neither grief nor love need solutions.[29]

There is no cure for grief, but it can be minimized through the loving support of friends and family, and I have been blessed beyond measure in this capacity. One card that I received when Mom died stands out in my mind. My grief was brand-new and accusatory. Why did God take her? Her neighbor's note reminded me that, like we do in a garden, He picks the prettiest and best flowers first. I would have preferred he chose the weeds, but it reminded me of Mom's beautiful legacy, her value "…far above rubies." (Proverbs 31:10). Simple gestures such as this provided impactful comfort.

My heart bears the scars of loss, but it also harbors tremendous love. Psychologist Joyce Brothers once said, "The best proof of love is trust." Trusting that our loved ones are pain-free, held close in the arms of Jesus, and we will one day see them again brings comfort. Grieving is loving, and loving is trusting.

Phone conversations with my children always end with "I love you." My mom and I said it every time we talked, and Elfie's little boy said it to him every night. Grieving those we lose means we continue to love them. Matthew 5:6 assures us, "Blessed are those who mourn, for they will be comforted." These are words we can trust.

---

[29] Devine, Megan. *It's Okay That You're Not Okay: Meeting Grief and Loss in a Culture that Doesn't Understand.* Louisville, CO: Sounds True Adult. 2017.

Mom, Aunt Martha, and Uncle Buddy

Brock

grind

/grīnd/

verb
1.

    a. reduce (something) to small particles or powder by crushing it.

    b. "grind some black pepper over the salad."

2.

    c. rub or cause to rub together gratingly.

    d. "mountain ranges developed along fault lines where tectonic plates ground against one another."

noun
1.

    e. a crushing or grating sound or motion.

    f. "the crunch and grind of bulldozers."

2.

    g. hard, dull work.

    h. "relief from the daily grind"

"Life is a grindstone. Whether it grinds us down or polishes us up depends on us." (Thomas Holcroft)

The grind of motherhood can take us in either direction. It is how we reduce the grit to manageable pieces and hone the edges that make the difference. We must be willing to change our behaviors and act in accordance with God's will. It is "hard, dull work," but it is worth the effort to witness our children transformed into polished human beings.

The following chapters highlight habits and reactions to situations with our children that hinder their growth. In partnership with God, we can affect change.

The Aftershocks of Enabling

"Some firsts just happen; some come when I try.
Some firsts make me smile; some firsts make me cry.
But I knew at that moment that I knew all along-
That first things first happen when I'm brave, true, and strong."

My Brave Year of Firsts: Tries, Sighs, and High Fives by Jamie
Lee Curtis (author) and Laura Cornell (illustrations)

Meet Frankie, a little girl experiencing many firsts in her young
life. She exhibits bravery in trying new things, such as tasting yucky
foods, tying her shoes, learning to ride a bike, and, most importantly,
admitting when she is wrong. All these experiences helped her realize
that she can do anything independently if she tries hard enough.

Teaching a child to ride a bike is a lot like parenting. When we
hold on tightly, they will never fall, but they will also be denied the
opportunity to ride freely and explore all the world has to offer. If we
gently support them until they seem steady enough to let go, they build
confidence to ride further and faster. They may fall but also learn to
analyze and correct their technique. This reminds me of the proverb,
"Give a man a fish, and you feed him for a day; teach a man to fish, and
you feed him for a lifetime."

My children are grown and flown. Mostly. A son or daughter
occasionally returns for a tune-up or reset. My oldest son just turned 31,
and his brother and sister are twins, age 29. Reflecting on my parenting,
I confess to enabling with a capital "E."

When my twins gave up naps, it marked the end of any mommy
time. It also symbolized the evolution of power struggles. This
diabolical duo would climb out of their cribs, pull out every item of
clothing from their chest of drawers, and trash their room. By the time I
walked back in to *"wake them up,"* the room resembled the aftermath
of the apocalypse. I, the Enabling Expert, would put the room back
together again—every single time. Don't judge. With three kids two-
and-a-half years apart, I often defaulted to the quickest path to peace.

This was a game I played often. I failed to abide by the saying,
"Lack of planning on your part does not constitute an emergency on my
part." Forgotten lunches and backpacks miraculously appeared at

school. I frequently earned exemplary grades on "my" homework. And heaven forbid they should come home to unmade beds! You don't know what you don't know, but I know now that the consequences of forgotten lunches, incomplete assignments, and sleeping in rumpled beds would not have killed them. On the contrary, they would have learned some important life lessons.

Continuing these enabling behaviors fosters a lack of self-sufficiency and motivation, especially as they morph from childhood to adulthood. Problems that no parenting manual addresses catapult us into nightmares that we want to wake from. We resort to the rescue method, throwing lots of time, money, and worry into situations over which we have no control. Over time, it becomes apparent that enabling them out of messy situations is a study in futility.

The previous paragraph is remarkable for how often the word "we" is used when "they" are the ones who struggle. We are determined to do everything in our power to find a solution while they continue their paths of destruction. We ignore the instructions of flight attendants to put on our oxygen masks first because we know we can save them if we prioritize their needs. However, that oxygen supply is limited, and they will eventually have to breathe on their own. Because we sacrificed our supply, we can no longer help them.

In *Praying the Scriptures for Your Adult Children,* Jodie Berndt refers to parenting young adults as *"whack-a-mole."* You bash one pesky problem just as another one pops up.[30] Because we often feel like we are paddling backward without oars, "going with the flow," utilizing quick fixes for unsavory situations, is easier than fighting the current.

1 Timothy 5, Paul gives Timothy instructions about caring for widows. Widows over age 60 who have lived godly lives and have no family to care for them should be supported financially by the church. But younger widows should not be offered the same assistance for this reason: "They get into the habit of being idle and going about from house to house. And not only do they become idlers, but also gossips and busybodies, saying things they ought not to." (1 Timothy 5:13) Paul explains that older widows have worked and earned support, but younger ones have yet to learn how to care for themselves.

---

[30] Berndt, Jodie. *Praying the Scripture for Your Adult Children.* Grand Rapids, MI: Zondervan Publishing, 2001.

This logic can be extrapolated to our children. But does this mean we should cut off all support? Not necessarily. There is a significant difference between "supporting" and "enabling." One of my adult children has been shopping for insurance. His dad gave him some great advice, which he used. My husband supports him in this endeavor but does not enable him by doing it for him. He is providing him with a hand-up rather than a hand-out.

The line between supporting and endorsing is often difficult to discern. It is hard to embrace decisions that our children make when our "momdar" detects red flags and warning signs. But supporting is different from putting a big red bow on it. As Berndt puts it, "A blessing is not the same thing as an endorsement." I doubt Bill Gates' parents endorsed his decision to drop out of college, but they staunchly supported his efforts to start a little computer company. We all know how that story ends.

Galatians 6:5 says that "Each person should carry their own load." It has taken me a long time to realize that my children should do just that. I can't solve any of their problems, nor should I. We "reap what we sow" (Galatians 6:7), and they must tend their gardens, weeds and all.

"The Diabolical Duo"

The Beauty of Boundaries

"Some people love hugs. Lots of people don't. And lots of people are somewhere in the middle."

Don't Hug Doug (He Doesn't Like It) by Carrie Finison (author) and David Wiseman (illustrator)

You can high-five, low-five, side-five, double-five, or spinny-five Doug. But under no circumstances can you hug Doug. He thinks hugs are "too squeezy, too squashy, too squooshy, too smooshy." Doug has serious boundary issues regarding his personal space. His stance against hugs guards against physical encroachment. Boundaries also guard against emotional intrusions. Author Sarah Ban Breathnach explains: "Limits are the barbed wire of real life."[31] They protect us from unhealthy relationships.

The word boundary evokes an image of a fence line, a line in the sand to keep people out, even those we love. However, it is about preserving love relationships by not allowing their toxic behaviors to impact us. We can love someone without liking their actions, but we must also establish a place where we cannot tolerate them.

Author Lysa Terkeurst uses three words to establish and maintain boundaries: access, responsibility, and consequences. Denying access to oneself by shifting responsibility to another person unburdens us from guilt, blame, and, ultimately, the consequences of that person's decisions.[32] One can never change another person, so the relationship dynamics must evolve. Detaching with love ensures self-preservation while safeguarding the relationship.

God also established boundaries for us, His children, in the Ten Commandments. They were not meant as a means of control or punishment but as a hedge of protection by establishing acceptable behaviors. Breaking one of His rules puts us in jeopardy of a spiritual

---

[31] Breathnach, Sarah Ban. *Simple Abundance: A Daybook of Comfort and Joy.* Grand Central Publishing: New York City, 2009.

[32] Ettinger, Zoe. "Boundaries from a Biblical Standpoint: PW Talks to Lysa Terkeurst." *Publishers Weekly.* 26 October 2022.

death, but this loving Father assures forgiveness when we take responsibility for our actions and ask for His pardon.

His boundaries are also present when he says no to a request that does not align with His will. The intent is not to be ornery; it is to prevent our self-destruction in the same way we attempt to protect our children from their poor choices. As loving parents, we must set clearly stated, gracefully implemented, and consistently kept boundaries because what we allow is what we live. Ann Lamott sums boundaries up this way: "I didn't have to set myself on fire to keep them warm. No is a complete sentence." If they are cold, they can wear a coat. It is not our responsibility to make sure they have one.

Boundaries are essential in the game of parenting. Permissive parenting is the fastest way to breach the critical distinction between the roles of parent and child. We want our children to like us. Our eternal love is sacrificed for fleeting likeability. We can be fair or fun, but our authority is weakened once this parenting boundary line is crossed. Proverbs 22:6 reminds us to *"Train up a child in the way he should go; even when he is old, he will not depart from it."* And if he does, the boundaries of our hearts will remain intact.

Sure, I grieve when my children break through the protective fences that I have established, but God is in the border control business, and I pray for his interference at questionable crossroads. Regardless of their actions, my boundaries will serve to protect my peace.

"No Boundaries" Jackson Hole, WY

The Consequences of Codependency

"Sometimes I am very mad. I don't understand why you weren't with me," says Little Rabbit, "I worry you will go away again."

You Weren't with Me by Chandra Ghosh Ippen (author) and Erich Ippen, Jr. (illustrator)

After a difficult separation, Little Rabbit and Big Rabbit are together again. They miss each other, but Little Rabbit is not ready to make amends with Big Rabbit. His hesitancy stems from a desire to punish him, but Big Rabbit assures him that their detachment did not diminish his love.

This struggle represents a classic ploy of codependency. Big and Little Rabbit depend on each other's acceptance to validate their relationship.

Psychology Today defines codependent relationships as unbalanced, where one person is over responsible, enabling the other person to underperform and avoid responsibility. The dependent becomes stuck because the codependent person takes care of them. Codependent people are so focused on pleasing, fixing, and controlling others that they lose track of who they are, what they want, and how to be happy with themselves.[33]

Codependency mirrors that of addiction. Just as the person with an addiction craves and uses substances to cope, so does a person in a codependent relationship, except that the craving is for acceptance of another person. Codependency becomes a "mixed-up motivation to help," shifting from voluntary care to a "have to" service, borne of a sense of guilt.[34] With addiction, fear most often drives this relationship. We worry about what will happen to our loved ones if we don't insert ourselves into their lives. Hope remains within reach if we cling tightly but will quickly dissipate if we let go. Lying, either blatantly or by omission, about their behavior disguises the non-conformity of a balanced relationship. We smother rather than cover it with love.

These behaviors are well-meaning but unhealthy.

---

[33] Martin, Sharon, DSW, LCSW, "How to Conquer Codependency." *Publishers Weekly*, 20 October 2020.
[34] Rainey, Dr. Russ. "Codependency: What Is It?" *Focus on the Family.* 17 July 2019.

Codependency reflects an enabler's lack of self-worth when the focus is shifted from himself to another person. The attempt to meet unfulfilled emotional and spiritual needs creates a relationship that is not God-centered.

In the movie *Mean Girls*, Amy Poehler played the part of Mrs. George, a *"cool mom"* who allowed her daughter, Regina, and her friends to drink in her house and even offered Regina condoms when she brought a guy into her bedroom. Mrs. George displayed classic codependent behavior. She sacrificed her authority on the altar of likeability.

For the longest time, I had codependent relationships with my children. When they were happy, I was happy. When they were healthy, I was healthy. When they cried, I cried. My self-worth teetered and tottered in sync with their accomplishments and failures. Attempts to confront, control, and conceal their behaviors only shoved me deeper down the rabbit hole. I knew I could save them if I stayed close enough to swoop in, pick them up, and put them back together again. I didn't realize it at the time, but a codependent parent does a monumental disservice to her child's ability to develop coping skills and healthy relationships.

Saul, the first king of Israel, demonstrated codependent behavior when he took control of a situation the prophet Samuel promised to take care of. When Samuel did not show up at the appointed time, Saul, driven by fear, presented a burnt offering that Samuel had vowed to bring. By disobeying Samuel's instructions, he also negated God's will. (1 Samuel 13-15)

When we continue to throw out lifelines to our children to save them, we risk being pulled into the undertow. The situation is often too precarious, too deep, to find purchase above the current. Not only do they face the danger of drowning, but we do as well. In Galatians 1:10, we are reminded that if we are people pleasers, we are "…not a servant of Christ." The only codependent relationship we need is with God.

The Benefits of Failure

"And then I'll look at you, and you'll look at me.
And I'll love you, whoever you've grown up to be."

The Wonderful Thing You Will Be by Emily Winfield Martin

All mothers can relate to this book's theme of our hopes for our children. It also reminds us that those same children belong to God first and foremost, and our expectations will never align perfectly with His plans.

While teaching kindergarten, the question "What will you be when you grow up?" always elicited entertaining answers. From the realistic ("a firefighter"), the fantastical ("a mermaid"), the comical ("tattoo artist"), and head-scratching ("a fire hydrant"), their responses revealed the creative inner workings of a five-year-old brain. But I can almost one hundred percent guarantee that these ambitions did not correlate with those of their mothers.

I say this with authority as I am one of them. As a perfect mom raising perfect children, I harbored smug ideations that all three of my children would navigate the path I had charted for them with no deviations. This perfect mom had to eat a little crow. That crow leaves an incredibly bitter taste when others are dining on Coq au Vin.

Let me clarify that previous paragraph. My children are kind, talented, and funny people. They are not following my life scripts for them, but they are doing life in ways I would have never imagined. God's plan was better suited for their gifts than mine.

As mothers, we cannot help but compare our children to others, especially amid social media options that lure us into juxtaposing our children's accomplishments against their peers. However, social media offers the highlight reels of life and not the daily mental and physical struggles. And, anyway, who has time to follow parenting fails and successes when we are just trying to keep up with the Kardashians and trolling Traylor? (Travis Kelce and Taylor Swift, for readers living under a rock.)

We nurture dreams for our children before birth, carefully

mapping the dots to align a promising future. As they grow, we begin to anguish when those dots are morbidly misaligned and appear headed nowhere. However, we must remember that failure is not a lack of success but an integral component. A newspaper editor once told Walt Disney he "lacked imagination and had no good ideas." Dr. Seuss' first twenty-seven book proposals were rejected. After his first performance at the Grand Ole Opry, Elvis Presley was told, *"You ain't goin' nowhere, son. You ought to go back to drivin' a truck."* Talk about eating crow.

There is no better example of turning setbacks into success than King David. David coveted Uriah's wife, Bathsheba. He committed adultery with her, lied to Uriah, and eventually had him murdered. But the prophet Nathan confronted David about his indiscretions, and David repented and begged for forgiveness. Despite these peccadillos and the loss of his son that he conceived with Bathsheba, he loved the Lord and did his best to honor him. No matter the circumstance, he always prayed to God for guidance, prompting God to proclaim this harpist and giant slayer "a man after God's own heart." (2 Samuel 11-12)

When we grieve the loss of dreams for our children, we must remember that if Jesus could turn water into wine, He can certainly perform miracles out of our children's messes. As parents, we must love them enough to give them the dignity to make mistakes. In turn, the lessons learned from these blunders build perseverance and character so that they also become people after God's own heart. As Ruth Bell Graham was often quoted, "It's my job to love and respect Billy. It's God's job to make him good."

Parenting is hard, but we shouldn't make it harder by trying to raise children who never mess up. It is about giving them safe spaces to land when they do without an "I-told-you-so" attitude. That is why we should set aside our grandiose expectations and allow God to do His job. Galatians 6:4-5 advises: "Each of you must examine your actions. Then, you can be proud of your accomplishments without comparing yourself to others. Assume your responsibility." Note that the verse utilizes "your own," not "your parents."

As author Sara Hagerty explains in *Is it Time to Bury the Dream,* it "might be at the gravesite of one of your dreams that you find the thing you want." And "the paradox of faith" is that "the death of what we cannot imagine losing…has the power to unlock the life we so desperately want."[35] When we take away that responsibility from our children, they become mired in a quicksand of stagnation and mediocrity.

We must teach and support our children, but they must navigate their lives according to God's plans. They may become firefighters, mermaids, tattoo artists, and fire hydrants. And that is okay. In a variation of a quote by Vincent van Gogh, let them dream of a painting, and then paint their dreams equipped with God's brush.

[35] Hagerty, Sara. "Is it Time to Bury the Dream?" *SOAR with Sara Hagerty*, 9 February 2023.

Empathy, Not Sympathy

"They have been so good to me," thought Hermit Crab. "They are like a family. How can I ever leave them?"

A House for Hermit Crab by Eric Carle

Hermit Crab has outgrown his shell. He finds himself a larger one, but it needs work. He meets new friends who assist him with his DIY home improvement throughout the year. A lanternfish provides light. A sea anemone improves the décor. A sea urchin volunteers to protect him. A group of snails agrees to clean. But by November, Hermit Crab had become too big again for his shell. When a smaller hermit crab saunters by looking for a new home, Hermit Crab gives him "the shirt off his back" on the condition that the new crab takes care of his friends. Saying goodbye to his old friends, he dons a new, larger shell, imagining all the possibilities for new adornments and new friends.

Hermit Crab quickly and graciously accepted his friends' offers of help decorating his new home. We could benefit by heeding his example. "I need help" are three words that are difficult to say. We do not want to appear weak and needy. Reaching out implies relinquishing control over the situation because no one can do it better than we can. We want to be the helper and not the one being helped. And more often, we don't want to be the spectacle, the spotlight, the sad soul that people feel sorry for.

After my mom died, my dad wanted to continue living in their home. He is legally blind, has no means of transportation, and is prone to falls, as evidenced by the numerous EMS calls made over the years. My brother is a single parent who lives near him but works full-time, and I live four hours away. We did not condone his decision but arranged to help him navigate his new normal. The experiment eventually failed, and three years later, he resides in an assisted living facility fifteen minutes from my house, where I can monitor his care daily.

But we both struggle in these new roles. Uprooted from a place he has called home for eighty years, he resents living in a place dictated by his health limitations. I empathize with his feelings and sympathize with his physical struggles. I want to support him but also foster his independence, which is not unlike my relationship with my children. However, this conflict of emotions causes me to tread the three bears' conundrum of too much, too little, or just right.

In Luke 5:17-26 we meet a crippled man who seeks Jesus' healing powers. People had swarmed to a house where Jesus was teaching, making the entry to see him impenetrable. The only access his friends could find was through the roof. They cut out a hole and lowered him down on his bed. Witnessing the faithfulness of friends, Jesus told the man to get up, take his bed, and go home. Instead of uttering empty words of sympathy, these friends empathized with the man's plight and took action.

The University of Wisconsin's Center for the Study of Pain conducted an interesting experiment. The researchers timed how long volunteers could keep their feet in buckets of freezing water. This led to a remarkable discovery: When a friend was allowed in the room with the person whose feet were in the freezing water, that person could endure the discomfort twice as long as he did when he was alone. The researchers concluded that "the presence of another caring person doubles the pain a person can endure."[36]

Whether it is someone struggling with addiction, a couple experiencing marital discourse, an elderly parent adapting to life without a partner, or someone with frozen feet, accepting assistance does not imply a character flaw or weakness. I always reminded my students to hold hands and watch out for one another on field trips, advice that should be extrapolated into adulthood.

But there is a caveat to lending support: People need empathy; they don't want sympathy. Support from an empathetic, emotionally connected person is invaluable. But if you have not had a similar lived experience, support may ring hollow. I heard the phrase "I'm so sorry for your loss" countless times when my mother died. While concern was well-meaning, I wanted to scream that my mother was not "lost." She was not a phone or a set of keys. On the other hand, when people wrote sincere notes of comfort or shared an anecdote or memory about my mom, their words comforted me.

Support can be tricky. As tempting as it is to give advice, we can't assume that we have it or that they want it. At the risk of dating myself, I recall the "Church Lady" character that Dana Carvey created

[36] Grieg, Pete. *God on Mute: Engaging the Silence of Unanswered Prayers.* Ada, MI: Baker Publishing, 2007.

on Saturday Night Live. In these skits, church lady Enid Strict interviewed celebrities in the headlines played by other cast members. Her initial admiration of their celebrity status would eventually segue into criticism of their secular lifestyles. The culmination of the interview was her "Superior Dance." We don't want to be church ladies. We can't assume we know what's best for someone else. Sincerity supports and comforts. Superiority does not.

I am a lot like Hermit Crab. My support system consists of a group of mothers with children who have had struggles like mine. In this circle, there is no judgment, only encouragement. These amazing friends support me when I need them. They also provide illumination, protection, and adornments of love and laughter. They clean me up when I find myself mired in the plough mud of parenting. They restore my soul as they "fulfill the laws of Christ and bear one another's burdens." (Galatians 6:2). I could not do life without them.

PATIENCE
Waiting is Not Wasting Time

"And they were happy together, waiting to see what would happen next."
Waiting by Kevin Henkes

Sitting on a windowsill, five friends wait expectantly for something to happen. The owl is waiting for the moon. The pig is waiting for the rain. The bear is waiting for the wind. The puppy is waiting for the snow. And the rabbit looks out the window because he likes to wait. Eventually, they witness the appearance of the moon, the rain, the wind, and the snow. They also experience the surprises of a rainbow and a new friend, a cat who has given birth to five kittens.

We spend much of our lives waiting, usually annoyed by the inconvenience. We "future trip," waiting impatiently with lofty, fearful, or unattainable expectations. The next rung in our ladder to success. Finding our soul mates. A cure for cancer or an addiction that is slowly killing a loved one. In his book *Waiting on God*, Andrew Murray endorses the belief that waiting for prayers to be answered "links us, in unalterable dependence, to God." By languishing in the space occupied by our longings, we may experience the "unbroken enjoyment" of his goodness.[37]

I don't know about you, but waiting does not fall under my bucket list of "unbroken enjoyment." For ten years, my husband and I struggled with infertility. I experienced numerous miscarriages while witnessing close friends add to their families. Attending baby showers with an empty womb only exacerbated my feelings of failure and hopelessness. While abandoning our aspirations would have been easier, we clung like gum to a shoe to our vision of a family. My maternal Timex clock was "taking a licking," but its ticking days were numbered. We patiently waited through exploratory procedures and tests until we had answers for my barren womb. Presented with undergoing surgery and infertility treatments, we opted in, although the process would severely strain us, both financially and emotionally. As a result of waiting, hoping, and praying, I gave birth to my first child four days before Mother's Day after a decade of holding space in the waiting room of hope.

---

[37] Murray, Andrew. *Waiting on God.* Fort Washington, PA, CLC Publications, 1999.

Sarah and Abraham were also barren. When God approached Abraham with the promise of a child in exchange for taking up residency in a new land where he would have more descendants "than stars in the sky," Abraham accepted the challenge, unaware that it would be 25 years before that promise was fulfilled with the birth of Isaac. Sarah and Abraham were the unfathomable ages of 90 and 100 when Isaac was born. I bore my children at ages 33 and 35, considered "geriatric" by the medical industry. If I was considered geriatric, Sarah must have delivered while on life support.

But Abraham and Sarah became impatient during those 25 years. Abraham made a costly mistake many of us make: He fulfilled his longing for a child using his own devices. Abraham had a child with Sarah's slave, Hagar. If this seems like a bad idea, it is because it is a bad idea. Abraham thought that this son, Ishmael, would become one of the descendants God had guaranteed. But because Ishmael was not part of God's bargain, his heritage was denied. There was no mention of having-a-child-with-your-wife's-slave in that pact. But when Sarah finally gave birth to Isaac, he became the heir apparent, as God had promised. (Genesis 15-22)

Jelly Roll (the singer, not the pastry) wrote a song about his tendency to look to God when his solutions to problems have been extinguished. The lyrics begin like this:

"I only go to God when I need a favor.
And I only pray when I ain't got a prayer."

What makes these plaintive lyrics more credible and relatable is his journey through addictions and incarcerations, seeking God only when hopelessness overcame him. His music reflects the pain of his past but also celebrates his long-awaited redemption by finding faith in his Lord and Savior. His years of suffering ended with a career in the music industry that has earned him reverent admiration and numerous awards.

I am not exactly the poster child of patience. My husband can attest to this character flaw if you don't believe me. My pet peeve is grocery store aisle hogs, oblivious to those waiting to wheel their carts past them. I also demonstrate impatience when making hasty decisions without consulting God. I enjoy giving God suggestions on managing my problems instead of waiting for his sound judgment and direction.

61

Ironically, the word "patience" is derived from the Latin word patientia, meaning "to endure, to suffer." No one likes to be in pain, but our good and faithful God allows suffering because He is teaching us perseverance to strengthen our faith. He also wants us to hone our requests to align with His perfect plan. Writer Anne Tyler admits that having children has slowed her writing ability. But she adds that they added "a dimension and richness to her offerings" that she would not have experienced otherwise. The same can be said of God's providential planning.

So, when tempted to take the easy route, the quick fix, slow down and consider the Lord's declaration in Jeremiah 29:11: "For I know the plans I have for you, plans to prosper you and not to harm you, plans to give you hope and a future." This verse does not promise a trouble-free life but, instead, the reassurance of hope. If we wait for his direction, we may discover rainbows, new friends, and the joy of God's promises.

Medical University of SC
Children's Hospital 1995

LETTING GO
Jesus, Please Take the Wheel

"'Fuzzy goes where I go,' said Owen. And Fuzzy did. Upstairs, downstairs, in-between, inside, outside, upside down."

Owen by Kevin Henkes

This children's book is about persuading a child to relinquish an item that brings the child comfort but is no longer ageappropriate. Owen's mom must convince him to surrender his blanket, Fuzzy, before he starts school. Her attempts are unsuccessful until she devises the perfect plan to cut the blanket into pocket-size handkerchiefs.

Like Owen, we all cling to things that bring us comfort and security. The physical trappings of life… cars, houses, and jobs…generate feelings of accomplishment. Relationships provide emotional security. We cling to and covet them until the car is totaled, the house is too much work to maintain, the job is unfulfilling, or the relationship goes sour. We refuse to let go of the things that are no longer satisfying because they are the things that once made us happy.

We just sold our eighteen-year-old family boat. The repairs required to make it summer-worthy were not cost-effective. But that boat represented so much more than a means of water transportation. It was a museum of irreplaceable memories. That fiberglass shell held flashbacks of my children coated in sunscreen and clad in life jackets as they were towed behind it on tubes, skis, and boards. Vacations and trips to Capers and DeWeese mark treasured time stamps on our family's lifeline. I have, however, tried to erase the image of them "air tubing." Once our kids learned that the momentum of bouncing the tube hard enough enabled it to become airborne, they literally took tubing to a whole new level. This adrenaline-pumping antic warranted the blooper show warning: "Do not try this at home." It was all fun and games until Patrick earned the broken arm badge of courage, reminding me of another famous line: "I saw that going differently in my mind" (Will Smith in the movie *Hitch).* I argued vehemently to keep the boat and make the repairs, but it would have been akin to putting lipstick on a pig. Like Owen's blanket, it was time to let it go.

Boats and children are similar in our attachments to them. We pay close attention to their needs, strive to maintain them in good

63

working conditions for ultimate performance and repair them when they malfunction. Boats are "fair weather friends," only worth ministering to when they are dependable, functional, and easily replaced. But children require a lifetime of faithful, not fair-weather parenting.

There comes a time in our children's lives when no amount of maintenance or repairs is necessary or helpful. Whether from simple maturity or a rift in the relationship, we find ourselves at the end of a frayed leash, not yet ready to cut the ties that bind.

If you have never felt like your child could not live without you, raise your hand, and congratulations. I have spent my entire children's lives trying to cushion the impact of hurt, hunger, failure, and disappointment. If I controlled what they did, where they went, what they ate, and who their friends were, success and happiness were inevitable. My hands were firmly planted on ten and two on the wheels of their lives, with Jesus riding shotgun.

Let's face it: Our adult children have free will and aren't afraid to use it. When locked into a push-pull relationship, we set ourselves up for a world of anger, disappointment, and resentment. According to author Jim Burns in *Doing Life with Your Adult Children: Keep Your Mouth Shut and the Welcome Mat Out* (best book title ever, in my opinion), if we can't control their behaviors, we must change ours. Burns advises us to "change our job description" from player to cheerleader. Deviate from treating them as adult children (an oxymoron if you ask me) to treating them as adults. "Hard as it is, the role you play in your children's lives must diminish for them to transition from adolescence to responsible adulthood." [38]

The Bible talks about "exasperating" our kids by not disciplining them and allowing them an unfettered life instead of bringing them up in the training and admonition of the Lord. (Ephesians 6:4) Freedom allows exploration and creativity but must be portioned conservatively and with set boundaries. On the other hand, when we exercise too much control, we contradict the Bible's declaration of being "fearfully and wonderfully made." (Psalm 139:16). We will never change one of God's designs, so we must meet Him in the middle of control and acceptance. Whether a child has a disability, an extra chromosome, a chronic illness, or has succumbed to the

---

[38] Burns, Jim. *Doing Life with Your Adult Children: Keep Your Mouth Shut and the Welcome Mat Out.* Grand Rapids, MI: Zondervan, 2019.

ravages of drugs and alcohol, acknowledgment of imperfections conveys acceptance and trust in God's sovereignty.

A famous artist once revealed this: "My mother said to me, 'If you become a soldier, you'll be a general; if you become a monk, you'll end up as the pope.' Instead, I became a painter and wound up as Picasso." Many of Picasso's eclectic contributions to the art world, notably the Red and Blue periods, can be attributed to the ravages of mental illness. This affliction was channeled into the creation of stunning masterpieces. Thank goodness he didn't listen to his mother.

Loosening the grip on our children's lives is especially painful when there is illness involved. In *The Heart of Addiction,* Mark Shaw addresses the secular versus the spiritual platforms of treating addiction. Shaw refutes the claim by secular platforms that addiction is incurable, creating a sense of hopelessness. But when identified as a "sin of nature," redemption from the ravages of the disease is possible. Hope is found. "Transformation" replaces "Recovery". Recovery implies returning to the person you were, but transformation promises a new creation in Christ.[39] We can support our children's recovery from the physical manifestations of their illnesses, but only God can facilitate the transformation. We must let go and rest in the hope and reassurance that God's map has a destination. The waypoints and ETAs may be undefined, but the ultimate destination is assured.

We must take our hands off the wheel and let Him drive.

---

[39] Shaw, Mark. *The Heart of Addiction.* Newburyport, MA: Focus Publishing, 2008.

God Provides Needs, Not Wants

"I have a dream about those shoes. Black high-tops. Two white stripes. 'Grandma, I want them.'"

Those Shoes by Maribeth Boelts (author), Noah Z, Jones (illustrator)

All Jeremy wants is a pair of shoes everyone at school seems to be wearing. Jeremy's grandma says their budget only allows for needs, not wants. When his old shoes fall apart at school, he convinces his grandma to buy a thrift shop pair that is much too small. But his sore feet persuade him that his warm boots, a loving grandma, and the chance to help a friend have greater value than shoes.

"Sometimes, you get what you want. Other times, you get a lesson in patience, timing, alignment, empathy, compassion, faith, perseverance, resilience, humility, trust, meaning, awareness, resistance, purpose, clarity, grief, beauty, and life. Either way, you win." (yung pueblo)

Or, in the immortal words of The Rolling Stones, "You can't always get what you want. But if you try sometimes, you get what you need."

This song was featured in the 1983 movie *The Big Chill,* in which a group of friends reunite at the funeral of one of their members to mourn his suicide. As the attendees prepare to leave, they nod their wry acknowledgment when Karen begins playing this song, Alex's favorite, on the organ.

The connection of this song to Alex's death has always confused me. Did Alex not get what he wanted, so he took his life? Did death meet a need he could not attain otherwise? Did he even "try sometime"? Perhaps I'm overthinking it, and this was his go-to song. But still...

All my life, I have been a classic overachiever. If I wanted it, I got it. Once I set my sights on a goal, my efforts became laser focused on the outcome. My school report cards indicated flawless academic performance and behavior befitting an audience with the queen. In high school, I became the first sophomore to win a spot on the Varsity cheerleading squad and the youngest to win the Miss Berea High School title. I finished high school with a 4.2 GPA and enough AP credits to skip an entire semester of college at USC, finishing in three and a half years. I wasn't the most intelligent, most athletic, or the prettiest. I just worked my butt off.

My winning streak hit the skids during my senior year in college when I met my future husband. We were a study in contrast. His favorite hangout was the Library Club, where drinks were poured loose and often, while I preferred the academia of the building that housed books. The man bought his writing assignments; I researched, indexed, and prepared my papers with military precision. But under his tutelage, my goal of earning A's spiraled into fun-seeking adventures as we dove into the underbelly of Animal House antics.

I married my enabler, and we hit a ten-year roadblock together: Having children. As hard as we tried, it would not, could not happen. Attending baby showers with an empty womb rubbed salt in the wounds of my infertility. Hope blossomed with each positive pregnancy test but wilted with each miscarriage. We succumbed to the financial and emotional roller coaster of infertility treatments and finally got what we wanted: a son and, two-and-a-half years later, twins, a son and a daughter. Unbeknownst to us then, we had signed up for the rollicking ride of our life. Some days, we enjoyed the idyllic Brady Bunch-esque lifestyle; others presented like episodes of Fear Factor. We wanted children, but we certainly didn't need the headaches that came with them. Our expectations were for perfection.

Perfect. The unattainable condition we aspire to and think we will achieve when we have everything we want. Even Jesus said, "Be perfect, therefore, as your heavenly Father is perfect." (Matthew 5:48)

But when we dive deeper into the biblical translation of this word, it takes on a different meaning. Not perfect in the Barbie-pink plastic sense, but "whole," "complete," or "mature." This perfection can only be found by surrendering our material wants in exchange for a need for the nearness of God. In her book *Breaking Up with Perfect,* Amy Carroll cites this difference between our definition of perfect and God's: "Creating an image is measuring up. Living in God's image is filling up." [40]

I wanted children, but God stamped my timeline for bearing them much later than mine. Our marriage faltered during our season of infertility. God's way of preventing a fissure to the point of collapse was not adding children to the mix. I certainly did not want to endure

[40] Carroll, Amy. *Breaking Up with Perfect.* Brentwood, TN: Howard Books, 2015.

anything but the joys of motherhood, but God used the challenges to draw me closer to Him. I did not get what I wanted, but God gave me those valuable lessons cited in yung pueblo's quote. He "...satisfied wants that fit within his purpose and will." (Psalm 37:4). That is what I needed.

Living, Not Anticipating

"Everything that the light touches is our kingdom," he told his son. "One day, the sun will set on my time here and will rise with you as the new king."

The Lion King (Disney Classics)

In the beloved Disney classic, The Lion King, Mustafa tells his son, Simba, "One day the sun will set on my time here and will rise with you as the new king." But when the evil Uncle Scar banishes Simba from the Pride Lands, Simba worries that he will never return to fulfill his destiny as King. His friends, the warthog Pumbaa and the meerkat Timba, accompany him on a long, arduous journey, and "one day," his destiny as the new king is fulfilled.

One day. Two words pregnant with promise. When Mustafa utters them to his son, they also imbue responsibility and trepidation. Banished from his homeland, Simba fears lifelong exile but also the burden of shouldering such a tremendous obligation should he be crowned the new king.

One day. This is a time in the future we often refer to as future tripping. A more clinical term is anticipatory anxiety, worrying about something that hasn't or may not happen. Anxiety is the beast responsible for future tripping, and future tripping feeds the anxiety monster. It cycles continuously "when we lose the here-and-now for some nebulous what if down some imaginary road."[41]

My husband and I live on the Isle of Palms on the South Carolina coast. We enjoy sobering calmness for most of the year as we bask in all this beautiful place offers. But beginning June 1st, tthe official start of hurricane season, we suffer anticipatory anxiety relapse.

We have weathered a few storms. In 1989, living in Mt. Pleasant, we survived Hurricane Hugo with minor damage compared to others who suffered total devastation. Floyd caused a Highway 126 evacuation nightmare in 1999 when every living soul decided to leave at the same time, and lane reversals were not yet a thing. I suffer from PTSD, recalling my adventure with three young children and two dogs

---

[41] Raskin, Bonnie. "Worried about the Future? Why You Should Manage Future Tripping." *Institute for Educational Advancement,* 22 October 2021.

broken down on the side of the highway, necessitating a rescue attempt through back roads by my husband and his brother. It was not "A Great Day in South Carolina," Governor Nikki Haley. My personal favorite was Matthew in 2016, which coincided with my husband's need for emergency surgery. Left to my own feeble devices, battening down the hatches became a study in futility. Pete has been forewarned that the next hurricane threat will assure my need for "emergency surgery" as payback.

There have been others, and there will be more. This is why the H-word feeds the need of Lowcountry residents to clear stores of every bottled water and battery on the shelves. We prepare for the worst and hope for the best.

Anticipation accelerates worry like pouring fuel on a flame. After losing both of her sons, Naomi did not know where she would go or with whom she would live. She unselfishly encouraged her daughters-in-law to return to their families, but Ruth refused to abandon her. Instead of facing an uncertain future, she was embraced by Ruth and given a grandchild who would factor into the lineage of Jesus. Her worries proved to be unfounded. (Ruth 1:1-22)

Naomi's reaction to her situation comes naturally to mothers. We are caregivers and have no expectations of being cared for. And mothers possess an exceptional skill set when it comes to what-ifs. Pregnancy drives fear that the baby will not arrive with ten fingers and ten toes. What-to-expect books exacerbate concerns when the child does not meet milestones on time. The pavement of school years trips the anxiety meter with underperforming grades and poor friend choices. And the journey into the teen and young adult years can be downright difficult. Anticipating what may go wrong threatens to steal every ounce of joy from a mother's bank.

But the road hazards and detours do not render our parenting journeys impassable. It's our dependence on guidance from artificial sources rather than spiritual divination. Our internal global positioning systems announce ETAs and destinations that often do not synchronize with God's. Anticipating the future prevents us from living in the present. In the words of Carly Simon, anticipation "…is makin' me late, is keepin' me waitin'". The doors to enjoyment stay closed as we dwell in the room of expectancy.

I sometimes pull a Marty McFly (from *Back to the Future* movie fame) and future trip in reverse. Had I chosen a different major/career path/husband, would my life look different? If so, would it make any difference? When my mind attempts to reverse or accelerate, I revert to the present day with blinders on, reflecting on the wisdom of Simon: "...and stay right here 'cause these are the good old days." As Matthew 6:34 reminds us, "Therefore, do not worry about tomorrow, for tomorrow will worry about itself. Each day has enough trouble of its own."

Spaghetti models, be darned.

"The Dock Days of Summer"

grace
/gRĀS/

NOUN
1. simple elegance or refinement of movement.
    "She moved through the water with effortless grace."

2. courteous goodwill
    "At least he has the grace to admit his debt to her."

VERB
1. do honor or credit to (someone or something) by one's presence.
    "She bowed out from the sport she has graced for two decades."

This acronym details the components of grace.

- G is generosity, the will to do something for others.
- R is respect, the dignity of life and work.
- A is action, the mechanism of change.
- C is compassion and concern for others.
- E is energy, the spirit that catalyzes us. [42]

The pressures of motherhood are daunting, but when we parent with generosity, respect, and compassion, we can affect positive energy and change.

Ernest Hemingway once said, "Grace is courage under pressure." When we give ourselves grace, acknowledging that our children are responsible for their lives, the pressures of motherhood become less restricting.

---

[42] Baldoni, John. "The Attributes of Grace." *SmartBrief.* 5 May 2019.

The Cleansing Power of Tears

"Tears help your mind, your heart, and your body feel new, clear, and calm after the storm. We need our tears, just as the earth needs rain."

Crying is Like the Rain: A Story of Mindfulness and Feelings by Heather Hawk Feinberg (author) and Chamisa Kellogg (illustrator)

A Washington Irving quote speaks to the vulnerability and sacredness of tears. "They are not a mark of weakness but of power. They speak more eloquently than ten thousand tongues. They are the messengers of overwhelming grief, of deep contrition, and of unspeakable love."

Translated, tears speak the heart's language, universal liquid words that defy interpretation or definition. They are "…words that need to be written." (Paul Coelho)

A 2016 *Time* article, "The Science of Crying," addresses the mystery of emotional weeping. While some species shed tears reflexively to signal pain or irritation, humans are the only creatures who cry in response to emotions, whether that be sadness, happiness, surprise, anger, or grief. Modern research is still in its infancy, but scientists have drawn one conclusion: "Tears are of extreme relevance for human nature. We cry because we need other people."[43]

In the movie *Cast Away,* Tom Hanks is stranded on a deserted island. The movie's dialogue is sparse, and the storytelling is dependent on the characters' actions and emotions. Hanks faces the daily challenges of survival using nothing but his wits, debris from the plane wreckage, and the natural resources of the island. His resourcefulness and determination allow him to withstand the elements and nourish himself by hunting and gathering. But when his lone companion, Wilson the volleyball, drifts away, his stoicism dissolves into tears of grief. Hanks copes well with the physical and mental demands of survival, but the emotional obstacle of loneliness takes its toll. Even though there is no dialogue between Hanks and Wilson…we all know

---

[43] Oaklander, Mandy. "The Science of Crying." *TIME,* 16 March 2016.

volleyballs can't talk…his tears reflect the research findings that people need people.

Especially mothers and their children.

My mother passed away on June 5, 2021. She personified the Proverbs 31 woman. Clothed in strength and dignity, she relied on her faith to live in the present and not fear the future. Her compassionate heart and good-natured spirit tempered her words. Our home was comforting and welcoming, and our table was always laden with nutritious meals.

And oh, my word, she was funny! Our daily phone conversations were peppered with family updates, gossip, and peals of laughter, often precipitated by another one of her clueless blunders. She provided unintended comic relief for our family.

Sometimes, her antics were wordless, like her attempt to order fast food at the silent garbage receptacle rather than the speaker, as Dad stifled laughter from the passenger seat. Or when she stood up in church to be acknowledged for her military service on Memorial Day. Mom was a lifetime bona fide civilian.

Then there were the classic one-liners. Shopping for Dad at a men's store in downtown Greenville, the salesperson presented a sportsman's vest used to carry ammunition and asked if he was a hunter. Mom replied most indignantly that no, he was a Collins. No matter how many times we rehashed these incidents, we would laugh until we cried or peed our pants. Or both.

That voice is now silent, and I miss its sound every single day. Memories of her bring a smile to my face, but in the words of Smokey Robinson, "…if you look a little bit closer, it's easy to trace the tracks of my tears." As described in the Irving quote, they speak of my "overwhelming grief" and "unspeakable love" for her.

Psalm 126:5 tells us that "Those who sow with tears will reap with songs of joy." This passage serves as a reminder that shedding tears of grief and brokenness can generate a spiritual harvest of understanding and peace. This last section, *Grace*, recognizes that finding calm amidst the chaos of motherhood is possible, much like tears provide relief for the soul.

I can no longer hear my mom, but my soul rejoices in her life and legacy. When a photo or a memory opens the floodgates, I imagine my tears watering that legacy to keep it alive. That hole that she left still exists, but my life continues to grow around it, much like the empty plans for my children are being filled with more vibrant and exciting ones of their own. We are moving forward with grace and an abundance of hope.

THE QUEEN OF MY HEART

For the Love of a Dog

"Once, there was a tree, and she loved a little boy."

The Giving Tree by Shel Silverstein

     The story starts with a boy and his best friend, a tree. The boy climbs the tree daily to eat the apples and sleeps in the tree's shade. The friendship becomes one-sided as the boy grows up, with the boy always taking and the tree constantly giving. Finally, reduced to a stump, the tree has nothing left to give when the boy returns, this time as an old man. But a stump is just what the old man needs to sit and rest. So, he sits, and the tree is happy.

     This tree is the bearer of unconditional love, a selfless devotion void of expectations other than making someone else happy. If you have ever owned a dog, you have been on the receiving end of this kind of adoration. Dogs think you are God, and they live to please you. Cats…not so much. Author Terry Pratchett explains: "In ancient times, cats were worshipped as gods; they have not forgotten this." As I write, my yellow lab, Lady, and my miniature dachshund, Gertie, provide warmth for my feet and heart. If I move, they become my ever-present shadows and go where I go, clueless and indifferent to where that may be so long as they are in my presence.

     We recently had to put down my son's lab mix, Folly. He was a rescue, so we were unsure of his age, but he had most likely achieved double-digit status. I do not think I have ever encountered a dog quite like him in all my years of dog ownership.

     When God was giving out looks, Folly missed the memo. Classifying him as a "lab mix" was a stretch. His beautiful yellow coat and happy disposition were the only identifiable characteristics of that breed. His eyes protruded in a most bug-like way due to a condition that rendered him blind in one eye and well on the way to complete darkness in the other. "Lumpy" was his nickname, a nod to the number of lipomas, or fatty tumors, on his body. But what he lacked in physical beauty was made up by a heart of the purest love, demonstrated by a tail that never, ever stopped wagging. Even when cancer impeded his stair-climbing ability, his tail waved triumphantly when he succeeded. When we found ourselves at the vet, doing the unfathomable thing that no pet owner ever wants to face, he continued showing us his devotion with that tail. Folly fulfilled his earthly purpose with loyalty and unadulterated love.

Mothers and Folly share a common characteristic in their uncompromised ability to invest themselves in others with no regard for the return on that investment. As the original giving tree, a mother loves her child with every fiber of her being, with no strings attached. This love never dissipates, even when the rough patches during the teen and young adult years can generate some serious unlikability. Author Jim Burns describes it this way: "When your children are young, they climb all over you and step on your feet. They step all over your heart when they are older and make poor choices." [44]

A mother's heart beats with the rhythm of her child, but when that child is out of sync, struggling with issues that we cannot control, the situation creates fissures that threaten the heart's health. Protecting it from a complete breakage requires detaching from the situational matters and focusing on loving the person with patience and kindness, not controlling or enabling them with anger and threats. When we separate ourselves from the face slaps of hurtful behaviors and disrespect, choosing instead to love unconditionally, we preserve the relationship.

There can be no better example of unconditional love than that of Jochebed's sacrifice of her baby boy, Moses, who, enclosed in a basket, was released into the Nile River to avoid the Pharaoh's decree that all Hebrew baby boys be drowned. Discovered by an Egyptian princess who raised him as her own, Jochebed was summoned to be the nursemaid. Unbeknownst to the princess, this was his birth mother. Baby Moses would grow up to be one of the most significant figures in Israel's history, the one God would use to deliver his people out of slavery. (Exodus 2:1-10)

I could not imagine allowing my child to ride in a car unrestrained, and it is unfathomable to think of strapping him into a straw basket and sliding it into the Nile River. But Jochebed's unconditional love saved Moses' life.

Mothers cannot strap their children in baskets and float them down the river to save them from the repercussions of bad decisions. A child's life rafts depend on his willingness to make course corrections,

---

[44] Burns, Jim. *Doing Life with Your Adult Children: Keep Your Mouth Shut and the Welcome Mat Out.* Grand Rapids, MI: Zondervan, 2019.

not our insertion into the situation. We must remember that their choices do not reflect our parenting but illuminate their communication breakdown with God. Corinthians 13:13 reminds us that we can only provide "faith, hope, and love." By releasing them to God's care, their footsteps on our hearts will not make permanent impressions. They will continue to beat like Folly's tail in time with our unconditional love.

FOLLY

The Challenge of Choices

"THEN...I saw a new kind! And they were good, too! How could I pick one? Now what should we do?"

What Pet Should I Get?" by Dr. Seuss

Jay and Kay, the kids we first met in *One Fish, Two Fish, Red Fish, Blue Fish*, reprise their roles, this time in a pet shop where they must agree on one pet to take home. The problem is, whenever they see an animal they like, they find another they like even better. The reader is left in suspense when the children emerge from the pet shop with a basket tied with a bow and two eyes peering out from under the lid. What choice did they make?

Oh, if only making decisions were as fun and benign as this. But choices often represent a fork in the road, and uncertainty skews our ability to discern the proper path. One road may beckon with instant gratification's bright and shiny promise, but it becomes a dead end. The other appears treacherous and unappealing, but it is worth the journey in the long run. In the words of Jerzy Gregorek, "Hard choices, easy life. Easy choices, hard life."

Take Jonah, for example. God wanted him to go and minister to the wicked people of Ninevah. Jonah wanted no part in this, so he set off on a boat in the opposite direction. God doesn't like it when we don't listen. God sent a storm as punishment, and Jonah was thrown overboard to stop it and prevent the boat from capsizing. Swallowed by a whale, God gave him three days in his belly to ponder his decision. When the mammal threw him up on the banks of Ninevah, he ceded to God's original plan for him. The people listened to his preaching, turned from their wickedness, and God granted them mercy. (Jonah 1:1-17) A cautionary tale, this story validates the importance of asking for and heeding God's direction when faced with tough decisions.

Jim Burns recalls this story: A young man asked an older man how to become financially healthy and responsible. The older man answered, "Two words: good decisions." The young man wanted to know how to make good decisions, and the older man replied with "experience." The young man's perplexed question followed: "But how do I gain experience?" The older man answered, "Two words: bad decisions." [45]

Unfortunately, our children often attend this School of Hard Knocks. When they absorb these lessons and make corrections, they graduate with high marks. However, those who fail to learn from these mistakes repeat grades year after year.

When our children are young, making decisions on their behalf, from the clothes they wear to the schools they attend, is necessary and crucial—but growing up grants emancipation and autonomy. Some of their decisions can result in poor, sometimes life- altering, outcomes. It is a chicken or egg conundrum. Without the lived experience, there is no teachable moment. But those moments can also inflict unsavory experiences, such as incarceration or health issues.

The problem with choices is that we can only see their impact from the rear-view mirror. We cruise along on decision-inflated tires until a tire goes flat, punctured by an error in judgment. But Sarah Ban Breathnach advises that bad choices should never be confused with wrong choices. She classifies bad choices as "coma choices" as they are often made without much thought to the consequences. In contrast, wrong choices are premeditated.[46] Writer Jeanette Winterson describes it this way: "Every time you make an important choice, the part you left behind continues the other life you could have had." We often cruise along with our internal GPS steering our route, unbeknownst that it is making coma choices in the wrong direction. And sometimes, it's too late to turn around.

Fear is often a determining factor in the timing of our choices. We put off making some decisions because they don't align with societal norms or expectations. To "go against the grain." requires courage and strength. It requires doing something unpopular or even despised because it is the right thing to do.

Many ordinary people have done extraordinary things because they made difficult choices. Rosa Parks' refusal to give up her seat on the bus ignited a Civil Rights movement. Nelson Mandela campaigned for justice and freedom to heal the wounds of apartheid. Martin Luther King, Jr. inspired people to fight for equal rights. Of course, these brave

---

[45] Burns, Jim. *Doing Life with Your Adult Children: Keep Your Mouth Shut and the Welcome Mat Out.* Grand Rapids, MI: Zondervan, 2019.

[46] Breathnach, Sarah Ban. *Simple Abundance: A Daybook of Comfort and Joy.* New York City, Grand Central Publishing, 2009.

choices did not go without consequences. Parks was arrested and fined, Mandela was imprisoned for 27 years, and King lost his life. But all three exemplified the words of Philippians 1:20: "I eagerly expect and hope that I will in no way be ashamed but will have sufficient courage so that now as always Christ will be exalted in my body, whether by life or by death."

I own some choices that I would like to have a do-over. Some were not necessarily bad, like choosing a college major that did not align with my skill set. There are others that I would like to purge from the hard drive of my memory. But, as Jim Burns reminds us, bad decisions enrich our life experiences if we learn from them and do not allow history to repeat itself. We will never experience the other life we could have had by the choices we made, but we will never lose the person we are because of them.

This can be extrapolated to our children. If you have a child struggling with issues that appear unsurmountable, remember that God's plan incorporates every experience, not just the good ones. My children's stories are still being written, but I have witnessed life altering situations that have affected the direction of their lives in ways I would never have imagined.

God has given us free will to make our own decisions. But he does not hang us out to dry when we struggle with a choice. Whether it is a pet or a fret, he wants to hear about our inner conflicts. We need to rely on Him so that our decisions align with His will, and then we can avoid poor choices, bad experiences, and challenging lives.

Roadblocks to Resolutions

"It's hard to be five. I'm little no more.
Good old days are gone. 'Bye one, two, three, four."

It's Hard to Be Five: Learning How to Work My Control Panel by
Jamie Lee Curtis (author) and Laura Cornell (illustrator)

      Change is hard for anyone. Especially a five-year-old. The
conundrum of choosing hard over fun challenges us from cradle to
grave. To forge the path of positive change often demands taking the
road less traveled and the least inviting. Flipping the calendar page to a
new year beckons change, but emerging from one's comfort zone takes
commitment and sacrifice, especially when the journey to positive
change is paved with potholes and pitfalls and rife with roadblocks.

      I have held a group fitness instructor certification for over thirty
years. To say things have changed in three decades is a serious
understatement. The era of leotards and legwarmers was a simple time.
We inserted our personally mixed playlists into the cassette player,
pushed play, and jumped and jived till our teeth rattled. Ironically, we
would take a thirty-second "heart rate check" every so often to
determine our rate of exertion. Weird.

      When change did occur, it was not always embraced favorably.
Participants were less than enthused by the introduction of The Step.
Replacing those high-impact, adrenaline-pumping high kicks with
slower-paced, low-impact, step-climbing eliminated the fun factor.
(Although many knees and hips thank us today.) Another adjustment
that could illicit downright nastiness is when someone arrived late to
class to find their coveted spot on the front row usurped by a newbie
who had no clue about the territorial rights of this band of eager
exercisers. This spandex-clad group presented a united front sadly
lacking in Southern hospitality.

      Today, "push and play" has been replaced with uploading,
downloading, syncing, and sharing. Dependent on Bluetooth and
reliable Wi-Fi connections, we find ourselves dead in the water when
those stars fail to align. Add to this mix a decrepit sixty-three-yearold
whose mental acuity refuses to understand how "this is supposed to talk

to that" to synchronize mics and music. Staff avoids me like the proverbial plague.

Back then, class offerings were limited to "aerobics" and "step." Now, we scrutinize a myriad of possibilities with puzzling monikers. Titles like "booty sculpt" and "dirty dozen" more aptly evoke nods to porn websites than fitness classes. On a more positive note, the fitness clothing industry has made some efficient changes. Thongs (who thought that was a great idea?) have been replaced by "poly-dri" and "moisture-wicking" apparel and allow more booty coverage while sculpting said booty. As a result of these changes, fitness instruction is safer, more effective, and less prone to wardrobe malfunctions.

At one point a few years ago, the number and variety of classes I was teaching required an excessive amount of preparation. Drowning in learning choreography, maintaining certifications, and teaching time, I was the "jack of all trades, master of none." Throwing in my "real job" of teaching kindergarten and learning martial arts material kept me teetering on the perpetual edge of a full blown mental meltdown. There was also that annoying husband and three children who appeared like clockwork for food, clean clothing, and taxi services.

Then COVID happened and forced a reorganization of my priorities. Stripping away activities that left me mentally and physically exhausted helped me realize that my "full" calendar was not actually "full"filling. I didn't need to keep doing things just because I had always done them.

Many Biblical characters effectively implemented change with profound results. Abraham left the security of his homeland to guide the Israelites to the Promised Land. Mary accepted God's favor of bearing His son when she knew that a pregnant, unmarried woman would not be seen favorably in the eyes of others. While these changes were not physically painful (well, except for Mary...childbirth is certainly no walk in the park), they did wield psychological and spiritual discomfort. Abraham and Mary overcame the two significant roadblocks of change...attachment and fear...and altered the course of history.

At the beginning of every new year, tradition dictates making resolutions that necessitate honest self-reflection. Dieting and exercise top Google searches, but those are like "putting lipstick on a pig" when issues are deep-seated and even life-threatening. Breaking cycles like dishonesty and substance abuse require true courage, commitment, and a firm reliance on God's guidance. Even with His navigation, there will be regressions and relapses. But these don't signify the road's end but offer the opportunity to reassess the direction and keep moving forward. In the words of author Terry McMillan, "Can't nothing make your life work if you aren't the architect."

In her book, *It's Not Supposed to Be This* Way, Lysa Terkeurst gives a beautiful analogy of how change can make us stronger. She explains that when the "grog," or the dust of a broken pottery shard, is merged with new clay, a stronger vessel can be fired at much hotter temperatures. People are like that. By incorporating the "grog," the imperfections, and the unappealing scraps of our lives back into our "vessels," the heat applied creates a more substantial and beautiful product.

Change does come with one caveat, as Sara Hagerty explains: "There is a thin line between strategies for improvement and strategies that disrupt the life God has placed for us." [47] Ephesians 4:22-24 defines positive change this way:" You were taught, with regard to your former way of life, to put off your old self, which is being corrupted by its deceitful desires; to be made new in the attitude of your minds; and to put on the new self, created to be like God in true righteousness and holiness."

Diet and exercise improve our physical health, but our spiritual well-being depends on feeding and flexing our souls.

---

[47] Hagerty, Sara. *The Gift of Limitations: Finding Beauty in Your Boundaries.* Grand Rapids, MI: Zondervan, 2024.

Acceptance is a Small, Quiet Room

"School is no place for me," said Chrysanthemum. "My name is too long. It scarcely fits on my name tag. And I'm named after a flower!"

Chrysanthemum by Kevin Henkes (Henkes, 2008)

Chrysanthemum is a mouse who is excited about starting school. Or she was until her classmates began teasing her about her long and flowery name. But when the school's music teacher tells the class that her name is Delphinium, Chrysanthemum finds her kindred spirit. When the pregnant music teacher announces that she will name her baby Chrysanthemum, the other students also want long and pretty names.

Unless you possess confidence with a capital C, you will eventually experience the Chrysanthemum Syndrome. Conformity ensures our kinship with one another, while differences set us apart. We are conflicted when choosing between fitting in and embracing our authenticity.

I recently read an article that addressed the connection between acceptance and happiness. When disciples asked a guru how to lead a successful life, he tasked them to pluck the largest sunflower in the line allotted to them in a set amount of time. But he set forth one condition: The students could not go back and pick a flower they had seen before but had to go in a straight line and a single direction. Their choices were intriguing.

Few chose the first big flower they saw for fear a larger one would appear later, but some plucked the first large one they saw and later wondered if they had acted too hastily. A few came back empty-handed because they could not decide. Others got frustrated when they could not find a bigger flower than the first one and returned with a smaller flower they plucked in the middle of their journey. A handful of them found the perfect flower but exceeded the time limit.

When the guru recognized the disappointment on his disciples' faces, he announced another round with a separate set of rules. This time, the only stipulation was to find the most beautiful and elegant flower. When they returned with their flowers, the variety was wide ranging: Large, small, tall, short, single stems, and multi-petalled. But the most telling of the experiment's success was the obvious delight of the disciples with their choices.[48]

This exercise summarizes the power of acceptance in our lives and highlights the contradiction between living large and living fully. When we continue to seek more, we often settle for less. However, "the moment we learn to accept that the flower in the hand is the biggest and most elegant one is the day when our lives change."[49]

On a random note, try explaining acceptance to a classroom of kindergarteners where chocolate and vanilla cupcakes are distributed vicariously. Be prepared for a full-blown meltdown of a five-year-old in possession of a flavor he does not like.

There is no finer example in the Bible of acceptance than Jesus' acknowledgment that he would be put to death. His incredulous disciples listened to him predict his fate. (Matthew 16:21-28) Jesus had free will, but He chose his Father's by saying "…not my will, but yours be done." (Luke 22:42) He accepted his Father's request that would cost him his life. By embracing his destiny, our own lives were forever changed.

As parents, we want our children to be the garden's prettiest, tallest, or smartest flowers. We know they will succeed beyond our wildest dreams if we provide enough sun, water, and fertilizer. But God is the master gardener, and we can only offer supplements to encourage and stimulate their growth.

Our children flourish best when not pressured by our unrealistic expectations but assured by our acceptance of God's plan for them. We do this by reminding them of this verse: "Trust in the Lord with all your heart and lean not on your own understanding; in all your ways submit to him, and he will make your paths straight." (Proverbs 3:5-6)

If you are reading this as the parent of a child riding the struggle bus of poor decision-making, you are probably confused. Does this mean I must accept my child's poor choices? Condoning this behavior belies every instinct of parenting. But condoning alludes to endorsement; accepting implies acknowledgment. Big difference. We can accept the situation without a stamp of approval.

---

[48] Yalameli, Chinmay. "Acceptance and Happiness." *Medium,* 6 October 2020,

[49] Gajadin, Vanayak. "Acceptance is the Key to Happiness. Why Trying to be Happy is Pointless." *Medium,* 1 August 2017.

Cheryl Strayed defines acceptance this way: "Most things will be okay eventually, but not everything will be. Sometimes, you'll put up a good fight and lose. Sometimes, you'll hold on really hard and realize there is no choice but to let go. Acceptance is a small, quiet room." [50] If we cling to the hope that things will be okay in this tiny space, that room becomes a haven of acceptance, peace and understanding.

ACCEPTANCE AT ITS FINEST

[50] Strayed, Cheryl. *Tiny Beautiful Things: Advice on Life and Love from Dear Sugar.* New York City, Vintage, 2012.

Humility Hero

"And today the great Yertle, the marvelous he, is King of the Mud, that is all he can see.
As turtles, and maybe all creatures, should be."

Yertle the Turtle by Dr. Seuss

Yertle is the king of all turtles, but his kingdom only expands as far as he can see. He orders his subjects to stack up underneath him, allowing for a better vantage point from which to rule. But his proud and greedy heart leads to his demise.

Yertle is not a humble turtle. He literally steps all over others to get what he wants. Humility is a trait we want our children to have and during a recent conversation with my oldest son, I recognized this characteristic in him.

After a bout with substance abuse, he is six years sober. A hot mess is the only way to describe his former self.

This son was pulled over doing 104 at 3:00 AM on the Ravenel Bridge, later expressing amazement that law enforcement worked at that ungodly hour.

This is the child that I had to take to college summer school in my Honda minivan when his "liquor sickle" got stolen. (Moped for those not well versed in driver-license-point-challenged transportation alternatives.)

This free spirit surprised us one morning with a note on the kitchen counter informing us that he had flown to Kaui to find a job on a horse farm for the winter. That we were surprised is an understatement.

This is the adventurous soul who joined a friend in Jackson Hole for three summers to guide tourists on horseback up the mountain trails of the Tetons. They had never ridden a horse before this adventure. Go figure.

This is the one who decided it was a great idea to rescue a fawn that had strayed from its mother in the Francis Marion Forest and take it *into* the nearby grocery store to purchase a baby bottle and milk. Legalities aside, this decision highlighted the lack of maturation of his brain's pre-frontal cortex.

This adrenaline-fueled junkie is why my hair is gray.

But today, he is married and relishes a life with horses and hard work. One day, he called me, his excitement in his voice reminiscent of his younger years, when every day seemed to hold a new adventure. He was back on a dirt bike track for the first time in five years.

When they were growing up, my husband and our two sons spent almost every weekend dirt biking. Some of our vacations were geared around this hobby, much to my and my daughter's chagrin. They had a fancy tow-behind camper called a "toy hauler," top-of-the-line bikes, and all the riding gear known to man. To an outsider, they projected the image of dirt-biking professionals (which they most certainly were not). No expense was spared on this "hobby" of the Page Brothers, more commonly known in the racing world as #007 and #427.

But today, when Pete called, there was no mention of these "things." On a twelve-year-old bike that he reassembled after years in storage, clothed in avocado green riding gear that had once belonged to his dad, and hauling bike and gear in an ancient Suburban that is practically held together by duct tape and has not seen a bath since it was manufactured, he was creating childhood memories that brought him so much joy. And that joy was palpable in our conversation as it traveled from Virginia to South Carolina. It was not reminiscent of the old days when his entitled self would pout for hours after an inferior performance. Instead, he laughed at himself as he recounted his next-to-last-place finish, and the comments other riders made about his "vintage" riding gear.

The Bible is filled with humble people. John the Baptist was a colorful character, but aside from eating bugs and hanging out in the wilderness, this cousin of Jesus was quick to give Jesus the glory as John's ministry waned and Jesus' was on the rise. When questioned about the new preacher in town and his rising popularity, he replied that "he must increase, but I must decrease." (Matthew 3:30). He accepted his demotion, so to speak, and humbled himself to the situation.

During our conversation I realized that Pete's concern for appearances had decreased in deference to his inner fulfillment. The thrill in Pete's voice made my heart happy, but his lack of caring about what others thought brought me tremendous pride. It is in moments like these that we experience the rewards of motherhood.

Mothers are the humblest creatures I know. We often sacrifice our hopes, dreams and needs for those of our children. Mothers lend credence to the C. S. Lewis quote, "Humility is not thinking less of yourself but thinking of yourself less."

We must also humble ourselves to the diminishing roles in their lives, just like John the Baptist when Jesus became the new preacher in town. As they move from egocentric toddlers to independent adults, we can continue to influence this trait by modeling compassion and gratefulness. They will be more likely to become humble people if they observe our appreciation for our avocado green vintage riding gear.

PAGE BROTHERS RACING "PROFESSIONALS"

Finding Dignity at the Dojo

"I'm gonna like me when my answer is wrong, like thinking my ruler was ten inches too long."

I'm Gonna Like Me: Letting Off a Little Self-Esteem" by Jamie Lee Curtis (author) and Laura Cornell (illustrator)

A boy and a girl celebrate liking themselves no matter the circumstances. Their egos remain intact even when they make mistakes, sending the message to the reader that our dignities are preserved when we don't allow situations to hinder them.

Years ago, I made the casual comment to my husband that taking karate lessons would be fun after watching my sons move through the ranks. As the saying goes, be careful of what you wish for. Just when I thought he suffered from selective hearing, he did not. That Christmas, I received a gift certificate for lessons and soon found myself clad in a crisp white gi, looking more like a fearful, wide-eyed nurse ministering to the war-wounded than someone who was geared for hand-to-hand combat.

As an avid exerciser and fitness instructor for many years, I relished the physical challenges and mental benefits of learning techniques. But with each belt level, it became apparent that I had veered away from the yellow "belt" road and landed squarely in Oz, where nothing made sense. I now know why Dorothy so desperately wanted to click those ruby reds and go home. I found myself participating in a sport that often found me flat on my back in positions that negated every ounce of my Southern ladylike upbringing. "Slapping out" helped soften the landing, although my gut instinct whispered to slap the offender. When tasked with situational applications (using those learned maneuvers on partners), I broke out in a cold sweat, suffered heart palpitations, and looked in desperation for the nearest rock under which to crawl. There were many times I left that dojo with not only an aching body but a badly bruised ego.

I can't help but compare martial arts to motherhood. Both start with the basics: Martial arts with its stances and strikes, and motherhood armed with pediatricians and baby-whisperer parenting manuals. The complexity of karate increases with time, as does

91

motherhood as we cycle through the seasons of caring for our children. When we wander into the upper belt/teenage and young adult years, we often find ourselves in uncharted territory with only our wits to guide us. The bad guys become real. We find ourselves flat on our backs with the inability to save ourselves or them.

Two of the impediments to rising to the seemingly unsurmountable challenges of motherhood (and martial arts) are insecurity and pride. As a mother, I do not want to be perceived as someone who doesn't know what she is doing. When my kids are doing life by the numbers, my dignity remains intact. They are extensions of my capable self. But when Humpty Dumpty falls off the wall, and I can't put him together again, my pride also takes a tumble. Sometimes pride does not "goeth before a fall" but because of it.

The movie *Bad Moms* features three mothers, Amy, Carla, and Kiki, who struggle to measure up to the volunteer demands of their kids' school. It is both laugh-out-loud funny and soberingly serious at the same time. The familiar conundrum of seeking volunteer of the year status or settling for slacker resonated with me. In all honesty, being recognized as a "good mom" may have had as much bearing on my commitments as my contributions to my children's schools. Sure, I wanted to do my part, but doing so also fed my dignity.

Mothers can be their own worst enemies. Our egos inflate and deflate with the successes and failures of our children. We suffer from self-abuse caused by intimidation and fear that we will be labeled bad moms. As the character Amy laments, "At least once a day, I feel like the worst mom in the world, and cry in my car."

Here's the problem with pride. In the spiritual realm, dignity is tied to the biblical concept of glory. Not glorifying self, but God. When we stroke the false idols of ego and question our worth, our connection to and reflection of God is impeded. The simple fact that we are created in His image guarantees dignity as a birthright. In Philippians 2:6-8, the apostle Paul declares that we preserve our dignity when we "empty" ourselves to serve others with kindness. We give all the glory to God with our words and deeds and do not seek to shine the spotlight on ourselves.

Proverbs 31:25 proclaims that virtuous women are "clothed in strength and dignity," but some days, all we can do is muster mantels of weakness and shame. We must remember that we will never rise higher than the image we have of ourselves. When our reflections mirror those of God, our dignities are preserved. Then, we can walk into the dojo or any season of motherhood clothed in self-respect with our heads held high, knowing that we are doing the best we can with what we have been given.

NUMCHUCKS PETE

Gratefulness, Not Wistfulness

"I'm doing what you said, Mama," she said. "I'm counting my blessings."

The Berenstein Bears Count Their Blessings by Jan and Stan Berenstein

Sister and Brother always return from playdates with a "want worm up their butt", as my mother used to say. Their lists usually include "Bearbie" dolls and the newest, hottest video games. But when a thunderstorm approaches, and they find themselves safe with Mama and Papa in their cozy home, the children realize they have everything they need, and those lists become superfluous.   The 400th anniversary of the first Thanksgiving was celebrated in 2023. The 1621 feast between the Pilgrims and the Wampanoag Native Americans celebrated the fruits of their labor after a long, hard winter.

To establish hospitable living quarters and produce enough food to sustain them was grueling work, and pilgrim children were not exempt. Their limited playtime existed of strategic learning games like "Draughts" (aka Checkers), "Naughts and Crosses" (aka Tic-Tac-Toe), and Marbles. Pilgrim girls played hopscotch and cuddled their handmade cornhusk dolls. They certainly didn't face hours of mind-numbing screen time and immerse themselves in the perfect, plastic, pink world of Barbie (or "Bearbies," as Sister might say). Pilgrim children knew nothing of entitlement. They were content with their rudimentary toys and happy for any time to play with them.

Present-day Thanksgivings provide a stark contrast. Today's cornucopias, befittingly known as horns of plenty, runneth over. Mealtime overindulgences produce food-induced power naps during marathon football-watching sessions. Leftovers continue to nourish us for a couple of days but eventually find their way to the garbage disposal. The fact that more than 333 million people faced acute levels of food insecurity in 2023 highlights the wastefulness of this holiday. [51]

The late humorist Erma Bombeck nailed it with this quote: "Thanksgiving dinners take eighteen hours to prepare. They are consumed in twelve minutes. Half-times take twelve minutes. This is

---

[51] "Extreme Jeopardy for Those Struggling to Feed Their Families." *World Food Programme,* https://www.wfp.org/global-hunger-crisis.

not a coincidence." We spend so much time and money shopping, cleaning, polishing, cooking, and baking, only to witness our efforts devoured as if this is our last meal on earth. Pumpkin and pecan pie triggered sleep energizes us for an early rise on Black Friday morning to fuel our overindulgent Christmases.

Maybe it's my age. Perhaps it's the curveballs my life has thrown me in the past few years. Possibly it's because my children are all grown and flown, and I never know who will be where on those magical days. It might be because I have no grandchildren to experience magic through their innocent eyes. Or, like that grumpy old Grinch, my heart has shrunk "two sizes too small." The holidays don't stimulate that preparation adrenaline like they used to. I no longer enjoy emptying those boxes of tired decorations and propping them around the house to evoke a false sense of celebration. But it has nothing to do with ungratefulness. It is that my life no longer necessitates these ornamental knickknacks to experience the joys of the season.

The Dalai Lama and Archbishop Desmond Tutu have survived more than fifty years of exile and the soul-crushing violence of oppression but are known as two of the most joyful people on the planet. *The Book of Joy* illuminates the wisdom and insightfulness of these two remarkable people. The focus of the Gratitude chapter centers on how our perceptions shape our attitudes about life. In a world of cup-half-empty and cup-half-full people, perspective determines whether one is simply accepting or highly grateful. In the words of the Dalai Lama, "Acceptance means not fighting reality. Gratitude means embracing reality."[52] We can begrudgingly eat burnt toast, or we can be thankful that our hunger is assuaged.

The story of Noah and the Ark is an enduring tale of sacrifice and gratitude. Noah and his family spent more than a year on a boat with a bunch of noisy, smelly animals. When they finally disembarked on dry land, Noah first gave thanks to God. In response to Noah's appreciation, God sent a rainbow, a sign that He would never again flood the earth. (Genesis 6:1-22)

Throwing myself under the bus, I admit to occasionally befriending the green-eyed monster. I have friends who travel, have numerous grandchildren, have impossibly comfortable lifestyles, and

---

[52] Tutu, Desmond, and Dalai Lama. *The Book of Joy: Lasting Happiness in a Changing World.* New York City, Avery, 2016.

never look like they just rolled out of bed (like me). However, some friends have lost spouses or children. Some are battling incurable diseases. Others fight daily to support children with substance abuse or mental health issues. A few are divorced and struggling as single parents. Pondering these scenarios through the lens of perspective, I am incredibly blessed and exceedingly grateful. Rather than simply accepting my life, I embrace it while remembering that "every good and perfect gift is from above." (James 17:19)

The pilgrims and Wampanoags endured hardships as they carved out lives 400 years ago, but they gave thanks for every kernel of corn that sustained them. It is easy to be grumpy when the Wi-Fi quits working or the car breaks down. But when we take a minute to remember our gifts and not our grievances, it helps to reflect on this Indigenous people quote:

"Looking behind, I am filled with gratitude.
Looking forward, I am filled with vision.
Looking upwards, I'm filled with strength,
Looking within, I discover peace."

THANKSGIVING AT KETTLEBRANCH RANCH 2023

Wisdom Through a Teachable Spirit

"So what will it be, Bear?" asked Hare. "The top half or the bottom half? It's up to you-tops or bottoms." "Uh, let's see," Bear said with a yawn. I'll take the top half, Hare. Right -- tops."
Hare smiled. "It's a done deal, Bear."

Tops and Bottoms, retold and illustrated by Janet Stevens

This old folktale follows a lazy bear and an industrious rabbit who partner in planting a garden. Each time a crop is planted, Hare asks Bear if he wants the "tops" or the "bottoms." If Bear chooses tops, Hare plants "root" vegetables; if Bear chooses bottoms, Hare plants "shoot" vegetables. Exasperated, Bear insists on tops AND bottoms, only to be given the silks and stalks of corn, while Hare scoops up the tasty corn.

This reminds me of a quote: "Being fooled once does not make you a fool. You only become a fool when you continuously fall for the same s(tuff)."

The biblical King Solomon was known for his wisdom, wealth, and writings. One of the most well-known stories occurred when he was a judge, and two women came into his courtroom, each claiming a baby as her own. When King Solomon threatened to split the baby in half, one woman quickly accepted his decision, but the other one begged the king to give the baby to the other woman. Solomon knew then that the second woman was the mother. (1 Kings 3:16-28) No coercion or threats were necessary to make his decision. He only used his wits.

There is a difference between being smart and being wise. Intelligent people are knowledgeable; wise people apply knowledge using good judgment. Lived experiences provide unique stores of knowledge, which are considered practical wisdom or phronesis. According to Wikipedia, "Phronesis is a type of wisdom or intelligence relevant to practical action. It implies both sound judgment and excellence of character and habits and was a common topic of discussion in ancient Greek philosophy."

I've met a lot of knowledgeable people in my time (as well as some who thought they were but were most certainly not). I've known wise people. However, one person whom I depended on for her practical wisdom was my mother-in-law, Lelia. Those mother-in-law jokes never hit their mark with me because she stood head and shoulders above the rest in terms of her quiet intellect and subtle advice. She passed away years ago, but her beautiful spirit still resonates with me. She was a natural beauty who took pride in her appearance, always neatly dressed and lipstick applied. Her grace and hospitality were always on display, and I learned many cooking and hostess tips under her tutelage. To this day, some of her recipes are staples in my cooking rotation. I did not, however, adapt to her self-help mechanic skills. She wasn't afraid to tackle a malfunctioning lawnmower, but I barely know how to start one. And I don't plan on learning anytime soon. I'll leave that to her son.

I now know that she also possessed superhuman strength. She lived years with a blood disorder, necessitating blood transfusions and treatments. Even in her weakened condition, she continued to provide her trademark Southern hospitality with no mention of her physical discomfort. There was no room in her pragmatic approach to life to allow a public display of her discomfort. She was not about seeking attention or pity.

When Pete and I hit a rough patch in the early years of our marriage, she did not take sides or spout advice. Instead, she quietly gifted each of us a Bible, lovingly inscribed with her love and support. She personified the term "class act".

Age and wisdom grow proportionately except when it comes to the maturation of a young adult's brain. That period evolves painfully slowly. It is like swimming through Jello slow. The brain is not fully formed until the mid-to-late twenties, so there is a lot of time for young people to make stupid mistakes. In tandem with insecurity and inexperience, immature brains drive unfortunate decisions.

The same can be said of us, their parents. Parenting manuals educate us, but lived experiences provide phronesis. The problem is we don't benefit from them until they are over. That is why listening for God's voice is so important.

Proverbs 19:20 tells us this: "Listen to advice and accept discipline, and at the end, you will be counted among the wise." We have two ears and one mouth. God designed us this way to emphasize the importance of hearing over speaking, especially when the words hold no value. "It is better to remain silent at the risk of being thought a fool than to talk and remove all doubt of it." (Maurice Switzer) You certainly can't do both at the same time effectively. God wants us to have teachable spirits, but when our mouths are moving with all the answers, our ears are closed to His instruction. We may possess knowledge and wisdom, but without teachable spirits, we will not learn.

It is said that wisdom comes with age, but it is our experiences that make us wiser. The depth of that knowledge depends on our willingness to listen to and absorb God's teachings.
In the wise words of Mary Catherine Bateson, "We are not what we know but what we are willing to learn."

MY MOTHER-IN-LAW, LELIA

Healing Through Feeling

"After a long, lonesome, and scary time, the people listened and began to hear and to see God in one another and the beauty of the earth. And the old turtle smiled. And so did God."

Old Turtle by Douglas Wood (author) and Cheng-Khee Chee (illustrator)

Set in a time when animals could talk, this beautifully written and illustrated classic children's book begins with the beasts arguing about their images of God. Their interpretations vary from a wind that never stills, a rock that never moves, and a snowy peak high above the clouds...until Old Turtle interjects that God is all these and "is." Then people are created, and the discord returns, more boisterous than before. When the dissonance becomes unbearable, an invisible voice yells, "STOP." The animals and the elements of nature remind these humans that they were put on the earth to promote peace, not chaos. The curative power of their natural surroundings calms the restless nature of the people, restoring balance to the planet.

This book dovetails perfectly with a recent *Time* article about the healing power of nature. When the Forest Agency of Japan advised people in the 1980s to take walks in the woods, called "forest bathing" or *shinrin-yoku*, Japanese researchers set out to discover the therapeutic benefits of this practice. They found that these walks promoted not only protection against cancer, better immunity, and lower blood pressure but also symptom relief of heart disease, depression, cancer, anxiety, and attention disorders.[53] As Hippocrates once said, "Nature itself is the best physician."

I am currently recovering from a traumatic spine injury resulting from a fall. My damaged cervical spine caused severe nerve damage and motor function issues. While my prognosis is good for a full recovery, this accident pressed the pause button temporarily on my over-scheduled life. Over the last month, I have been forced to put aside my to-do lists and table my calendar in exchange for activities bound by my physical limitations. While therapists devise plans to

---

[53] Sifferlin, Alexandra. "The Healing Power of Nature." *Time*, 14 July 2016.

overcome this trauma to my body, the unexpected gift of time affords me the opportunity to reflect on and rejuvenate my spiritual health.

Over the past few years, my soul has been battered and bruised from the loss of several family members, including my mother and brother, and the ravages of mental illness and substance abuse on others. There are no medications or cures for my damaged psyche, but the loving support from friends and family has brought peace and understanding to situations over which I have no control. I am fortunate to be part of a family that believes in the healing power of Jesus as they pray without ceasing. And the friendships that have been forged with mothers who share similar heartaches have been life-altering. These people don't just talk the talk but walk the walk because their footsteps have often traveled the same path as mine. As C. S. Lewis explains, "Friendship is born at that moment when one person says to another: What! You too? I thought I was the only one."

The Bible is rife with stories of Jesus' miraculous healings. The synoptic gospels, the books of Matthew, Mark, and Luke, provide 22 stories of healing. We hear about Jesus healing a woman who has bled for 12 years and restoring sight to two blind men. (Luke 8:43-48, Matthew 9:27-31) Lepers, cast from society because of their illnesses, are restored to health through Jesus' compassion. (Luke 17:11-19)

It is in the story of the healing of ten lepers that we witness the distinction between "healing" and "wholeness." After the ten men walk away, free of disease, one man returns to express his gratitude. Jesus recognized this extension of the man's healing as being made complete and said to him, "Rise and go. Your faith has made you whole." (Luke 17:19). The bodies of the nine lepers who walked away were cured, but the one man who recognized God's sovereignty and grace, experienced complete restoration of his body, mind, and spirit.

Mothers hide pain well. We affix bandages to our children's booboos while nursing bruises to our egos inflicted by parenting stumbles. Eyeglasses correct a child's vision, but hindsight never provides us with second chances to rectify decisions. Broken limbs supported by casts will mend, but our hearts suffer permanent damage from a child who has gone astray.

But it doesn't have to be this way. Daniel Bonhoeffer declares, "God will constantly be crossing our paths and canceling our plans." Especially if you have children, I might add. Recognizing that disruptions and parenting fails are not necessarily limiting but limitless is critical. Author Sara Hagerty refers to it as how we see the fence line.

Perspective "can reach into us, disrupt old thought patterns, and reshape the way we think." [54] When we follow the leper's example and acknowledge God's power to heal, our shattered mom egos are restored.

Our bodies and hearts have stories to tell if we slow down and listen, but the first step toward healing is feeling. When I fell, my hands and fingers suffered temporary paralysis. But as the days wane on, the tingling and movement I am experiencing signify an improvement in my condition. Soon, I will walk again on the beach with my dogs, putting into practice the Japanese theory of the healing power of nature. My movements will most likely return to normal, but I also expect improvement in my emotional and spiritual well being as I tend to my soul's longings. In the words of Ernest Hemingway, "The world breaks everyone, and afterward, many are strong in the broken places."

Mom's 80th Birthday Party

[54] Hagerty, Sara. *The Gift of Limitations: Finding Beauty in Your Boundaries.* Grand Rapids: MI, Zondervan, 2024.

Resting in the Shade of Spiritual Wholeness

"I get it," said Michael. "Maybe good luck and bad luck are all mixed up. You never know what will happen next."

Zen Shorts by Jon Muth

Stillwater is a giant panda who moves into the neighborhood and tells fantastic tales, based on Zen stories from China, to three of the neighborhood children. Addy hears a story about the value of material goods. Michael is taught a lesson about pushing the boundaries of good and evil. To Karl, he demonstrates why holding on to frustration is not a good thing.

Stillwater imparts his profoundly spiritual outlook on life to Addy, Michael, and Karl by offering them more understanding and kinder alternatives to materialism, boundaries, and frustration. This is a children's book, but it is also a thought-provoking read for adults.

According to Vocabulary.com, Zen is the Japanese pronunciation of a Chinese word, *ch'an*, which comes from a Sanskrit root meaning "thought," "absorption," or "meditation." A more common explanation is "being in the moment," a habit that promotes spiritual integrity. God does not want us to live lives regretting the past or dreading the future but to rest in the here and now of His presence.

I am writing this from my happy place. It is a perfect spring morning. Seated in an Adirondack chair on my deck, the communion with nature…the melodic language of birds, gentle breezes ruffling the elephant ear leaves, the slow-moving creek tide…feeds my senses and my soul. As my miniature dachshund naps contentedly in my lap and my yellow lab rests her big blockhead on the deck railing, surveying her kingdom, I wonder if heaven could improve on this. At this moment, I have found my Zen.

Over the past few years, this peaceful, easy feeling has often eluded me. Life has thrown me some curveballs that no matter how hard I swung the bat, I could not connect and knock them out of the park. Thought, absorption, and meditation were unattainable. The chance of Zen was zero.

Sarah Ban Breathnach reminds us of an Indian proverb that compares one's life to a house with four rooms. Those rooms contain the physical, mental, emotional, and spiritual facets of our lives. While we tend to dwell in only one room most of the time, we should enter each room every day, if only to air it out, to complete the puzzles of our beings.[55] My physical, mental, and emotional rooms kept me locked in, keeping me from entering the room I needed most: my spiritual space.

The same can be said of God. He holds the answers to our physical, mental, emotional, and spiritual questions. Psalm 73:26 reads, "My flesh and my heart may fail, but God is the strength of my heart and my portion forever," serving as a reminder that God protects the integrity of every fiber of our beings. When we find ourselves broken by disappointment, divided by indecision, or fragmented by fear, our faith reconnects the dots to make us whole again.

In Jerusalem, there was a pool with healing powers that the lame, blind, and paralyzed went to lie in to be cured of their afflictions. It is where Jesus met a man who had been lame for thirty-eight years. The man was growing frustrated by his inability to make it into the pool. When Jesus asked him if he wanted to get well, he replied yes, and Jesus told him to roll up his mat and go home. And he did. This story is found in John 5:1-29, and it is interesting to note that in the original King James Version, Jesus asks the man if he wants to be made "whole," while later interpretations use the words "well" or "healed." The critical difference between these two words is that to heal is to cure a current physical condition, while to be made whole alludes to the restoration of the soul. Both promote a return to physical health and emotional happiness, but being made whole incorporates the missing spiritual piece.

A quote by Parker J. Palmer imparts this nugget of wisdom: "Wholeness does not mean perfection; it means embracing brokenness as an integral part of life." In the words of Michael in *Zen Shorts,* "...good luck and bad luck are all mixed up". In life, we will have disproportionate doses of both. The lame man at the pool exchanged his misfortune for good health when he answered yes to Jesus' question. That is where our spiritual wholeness lies as well.

---

[55] Breathnach, Sarah Ban. *Something More: Excavating Your Authentic Self.* New York City: Warner 1Books, 1998.

HAMLIN CREEK, ISLE OF PALMS

Joy Dives Deeper than Surface Happiness

"Maybe you should try to forget about winning and just dance because it makes you happy!" said Grandma. "Dance for joy."

Olivia Dances for Joy by Ian Falconer

   Olivia's dance team decides to enter the annual Maywood Dance Contest. Olivia can't contain her excitement. Here's the problem: They must compete against The Prancer Dancers, a team that dances with military precision and wins the coveted trophy every single year. When Olivia's team expresses doubt about whether they should even try, Olivia convinces them that dancing is not about perfection but celebrating joy.

   As a kindergarten teacher, Olivia became one of my favorite book characters. She is an energetic little pig with a vivid imagination. The simple black, white, and red color scheme provides a stark contrast to her creative solutions to challenging situations. Her precocious personality and general joie de vivre captivate the reader.

   Our miniature dachshund, Gertie, bears a personality similar to Olivia's. Her curiosity and problem-solving skills contradict her size. If the toy box is too tall, she climbs in it. Sofas and beds do not impede her need for snuggles. She possesses energy on steroids; she does not run, she bounces. If she were a cat with climbing gear, she would scale my body in a skinny minute every time I walked in the door. On our beach walks, she has never met another dog or person she didn't like. We have had serious conversations about "stranger danger" and encroaching on people's personal space to no avail. A sunbather in a beach chair is a lap to climb onto. She is in her happy place as she unrolls yet another toilet paper roll or creates a minefield of squeaky toys throughout the house. A petite package of sunshine and rainbows, she exudes joy.

   We think of joy as a nebulous emotion, but the American Psychological Association attempts to explain joy in scientific terms. The APA defines joy as "a feeling of extreme gladness, delight, or exaltation of the spirit arising from a sense of well-being or satisfaction." It can be passive, content with the way things are, or active, wanting to share a joyful experience with others. In physiological terms, joy activates the parasympathetic nervous system, promoting "peace, calm, confidence, and self-esteem." In contrast, the sympathetic nervous system is activated by feelings of happiness, which we associate with "excitement, energy, and activity".[56]

The words joy, rejoice, or joyful appear 430 times in the Bible. The words happy or happiness occur in only ten. Joy is especially prevalent at the birth of Jesus. Angels brought "good tidings of great joy." (Luke 2:10). The Wise Men "rejoiced with exceeding great joy." (Matthew 2:10). The hymn, "Joy to the World," triumphantly heralds the birth of baby Jesus.

Christmas also presents the opportunity to observe the difference between joy and happiness. Children become giddy with happiness when making their lists for Santa and opening their gifts on Christmas morning. But re-enacting the Nativity scene, singing a melody, or choosing a gift for an Angel Tree recipient fills them with joy. Receiving a present brings happiness, but it dissipates once the novelty of the gift wears off. Doing for others fosters lasting inner joy.[57]

One of the biggest roadblocks to maintaining a sense of joy is our belief that it is temporary and that, at any minute, the world will come crashing down around us. In Sara Hagerty's book, *Adore*, she recalls a conversation with one of her adopted daughters who endured an early life of poverty. The little girl announces that every time she has a happy day, she gets "really afraid" afterward. As Sara reminds us, "It's too good to be true" is often our response to God's gifts. We forget that the same God "who doesn't just hold the files of our lives but writes them" wants us to be joyful and content. [58]

Happiness correlates with external events; joy relies on our inner peace regardless of those events. Getting a new job may make us temporarily happy, but we realize joy when we experience the intrinsic reward of being successful at that job. Joy dives deeper than surface happiness. As Sarah Breathnach adds, "We think that it's the big moments that define our lives—the wedding, the baby, the new house,

[56] *APA Dictionary,* https://dictionary.apa.org/joy.

[57] Eyre, Linda and Eyre, Richard. "Joy vs. Happiness at Christman." *Deseret News,* 20 December 2017.

[58] Hagerty, Sara. *Adore A Simple Practice for Experiencing God in the Middle Minutes of Your Day.* Grand Rapids, MI, Zondervan, 2020.

the dream job. But really, these big moments of happiness are [just] the punctuation marks of our sagas."[59]

Lately, joy often eludes me. The burdens of caring for an aging parent and supporting adult children who are struggling are weighing heavily on my soul. Navigating these uncharted territories is joy-sucking. But it is up to me to look for the light, the sunshine, the positivity of the day. In the words of Russell M. Nelson, *"The joy we feel has little to do with the circumstances of our lives and everything to do with the focus of our lives."* Perspective is the key to finding the joy overshadowed by reality.

The Dalai Lama and Archbishop Desmond Tutu remind us that "Joy is a byproduct of an open heart and an open mind."[60] Like Gertie, we must let no situation be too tall, too frightening, or too overwhelming. When we open our hearts and our minds to the goodness of God, we can find joy in any situation. As Thessalonians 5:16 reminds us, *"Rejoice always".*

[59] Breathnach, Sarah Ban. *Something More: Excavating Your Authentic Self.* New York City, Warner Books, 1998.

[60] Tutu, Desmond, and Dalai Lama. *The Book of Joy: Lasting Happiness in a Changing World.* New York City, Avery, 2016.

Appreciating the (Miserable) Good Times

"When summer began, I headed out west. My parents had told me I needed a rest. 'Your imagination,' they said, 'is getting too wild. It will do you some good to relax for a while.'"

How I Spent My Summer Vacation by Mark Teague

Wallace Bleef's imagination takes over in his essay about how he spent his summer vacation. Instead of visiting Aunt Fern, he insists he was carried off by cowboys who taught him everything from riding broncos to roping cattle. His reverie ends just as he arrives at Aunt Fern's in time to divert a stampede.

Wallace's adventures out west are purely fictional, but New Orleans is a place where fact often seems stranger than fiction. America may be known as a melting pot of diverse people, but NOLA, the city's familiar acronym, must stand for New Opportunities for Losing Apprehensions. It is ground zero for letting your freak flag fly.

A couple of years ago, my husband and I visited this unique city for the first time to attend a wedding. It is replete with diverse cultural influences reflected in its architecture, art, and food. But this Baptist-bred, conservative southern belle was not prepared for its debauchery. Strolling down the sidewalk often requires stepping over a body, sleeping off the excesses of the night, or inhaling the secondhand smoke of an "herbal" cigarette. New York may be the city that never sleeps, but New Orleans is the party-till-you-puke, all-nighters-on-steroids destination. Famous for its hurricanes…drinks, and storms…it is Disneyland for the Different.

This is not a place my family would vacation. Not because it is unwholesome, but because it is too much like…well, a vacation. The Pages are renowned for our untraditional getaways. Except for our honeymoon in St. Thomas a thousand years ago (and I still accuse my husband of false representation of the charmed life we would lead), all our "vacations" have included some element of adventure and little time to sip frozen umbrella drinks by the pool. We are weird.

Yes, we've done the Disney/Universal Studios thing. But visiting there with little kids is no walk in the park, pardon the pun. We've skied out west and up north, but that was also too much work and too cold for my South Carolina blood. Colonial Williamsburg and Cape Canaveral were educational, but it turns out cerebral experiences for the Pages are a waste of time. We just want to have fun.

But those are our "normal" experiences. Let's talk about our real non-vacation vacations.

Once, we spent a solid week in Georgia so that my sons could ride every dirt bike track in the state while the five of us and two dogs lived in our "toy hauler," a specially designed mobile home with the capacity to transport motorcycles inside. The only difference between our Noah's Ark on Wheels and the original one is that we breathed gas fumes rather than livestock emanations. Nori and I spent our free time scrubbing the red mud from their racing gear in a washtub and watching mind-numbing movies over and over. I never, ever care to see *Splash* or *Stick It* again.

Two separate summers, we traveled in our boat for a week each time, once north and once south. When I say boat, we are not talking about a luxury floating home. We docked next to some of those extravagant vessels whose passengers watched in amusement as we pulled our portable air conditioning unit from below and secured it on top so that we could sleep comfortably at night. We were the nautical equivalent of the Beverly Hillbillies. Nothing says family togetherness like three kids, two dogs, and one tiny toilet on a 26' boat, especially when the boat breaks down in Hooterville, USA. People have committed murder over less.

Perhaps my favorite was a trip to Jackson Hole, where my son worked on a ranch. He also planned our itinerary. Listen carefully when I tell you this: Don't ever let your wild child plan your vacation itinerary. After four days of horseback riding, whitewater rafting, and hiking nine miles up the side of a very steep mountain, we completed our visit touring the countryside in an open-air, all-terrain vehicle. I spent the whole day breathing dusty air and holding on to my helmet to keep my head from popping off. I could not wait to go home to rest from this "vacation."

We scalloped in Florida, where I had a panic attack while snorkeling. Our swim with the manatees produced no sightings of sea cows, but it did generate a lot of whining about wearing wetsuits in 90+ degree heat. On our budget excursion to the Bahamas, we stayed in a

110

home that required a dinghy ride to the mainland. Upon departure, we realized that all three kids had lice, so we left a host gift that would keep on giving. I will never forgive any of them for that ice bath tube float down the Ichetucknee River.

For a long time, Hannah's attempt to conceive was as futile as our sighting of a manatee. But finally, in God's time, she bore a son, Samuel, whom she immediately dedicated to Him in appreciation for His gift. There was no lamenting about the amount of time it took or the toll it took on her mental and physical health.
She said, "I prayed for this child, and the Lord granted me what I asked of him." Samuel 1:27.

Hannah probably experienced some of the same emotions as I did while "enjoying" our vacations. At times I was hot, cold, exhausted, frightened, or just plain pissed off, but there is not a spa, a frozen drink, or a long afternoon nap that could fill my heart the way these memories do. I would not trade any of these miserable experiences for the most exotic, expensive vacation on earth. If I never visit my bucket list destinations, I will die happy and fulfilled because we let our freak flags fly. We may be weird, but we know how to have fun.

Leaving a Legacy of Laughter

"Yes, only you haven't heard the bestest part yet!" I said very loud.
"Because guess what else? He's a MONKEY!"

Junie B. Jones and a Little Monkey Business by Barbara Park

When Grandma Miller is overheard describing Junie B.'s new baby brother as *"the cutest little monkey ever,"* she excitedly shares the news that her brother is a real, live monkey during Show and Tell. Her friends give her gifts so that they can be the first to see him, but her teacher insists that she give them back when this turns out to be untrue.

Moral dilemmas are the bane of this precocious kindergartener's existence. Her creative but frequently questionable resolutions provoke laughter at the expense of her poor judgment. While her hare-brained schemes entertain her young readers, they also provide subtle admonitions of "don't try this at home."

Junie B. provokes laughter during stressful situations, unwittingly demonstrating the phrase "laugh to keep from crying." Laughter often serves as a coping mechanism when our survival instinct demands any response but laughter. Our lives are filled with both heartache and happiness, and without experiencing one, we can never understand or appreciate the other. In the words of the late humorist Erma Bombeck, *"There is a thin line between laughter and pain, comedy and tragedy, humor and hurt. And how do you know laughter if there is no pain to compare it to?"*

When a journalist asked clinical psychologist Bryan Howes about the most surprising part of being a therapist, of helping people through some of the most painful places in their lives, he replied that he never expected to laugh so much. He offers Freud's explanation of jokes in times of stress as "the shocking, unexpected, vaguely inappropriate words or gestures that convey a feeling that many have, but few people act upon."[61] When told that she would give birth at 90 years of age, Sarah laughed incredulously. She laughed again, this time with happiness, when Isaac was born, proving the duplicity of this emotion.

---

[61] Howes, Ph.D., Bryan. "Laughter in Therapy." *Psychology Today*, 31 December 2013.

Howes' observation is evident in a support group that I attend. Laughter and bleep-worthy language when no other words pack an adequate punch often permeate our meetings as we commiserate about the absence of brain cells of our children. More than once, a new member has expressed surprise that our meetings resemble more of a celebration of life than a funeral dirge. As Howes points out, levity forms bonds from the "meaningful moments of empathy and insight." We form alliances over shared experiences, and levity eases the constrictive nature of these ties.

My mom and her sister, Aunt Martha, took laughing inappropriately to a whole new level. Their mishaps and ensuing peals of laughter were renowned at their church and in their community. They were Lucy and Ethel on steroids.

They were famous for their "be back in a minute" statements, only to reappear hours later with many bags in tow, usually impulse sale items. I once asked Mom what something cost that she was headed to the register to buy. She replied that she didn't know, but it was on sale.

Another time, as they stood in the receiving line of a funeral, Aunt Martha introduced herself first. Mom, whose name is Patricia, was next and introduced herself as Martha as well. This, of course, was followed by a socially unacceptable fit of laughter. Situations that would embarrass most people, like mistakenly getting in a car with a stranger at church or leaving the car running as they shopped, would set them off. I can't tell you how many times my mom peed her pants in public.

My mother was my idol when it came to laughing in the face of adversity. Her faith was impenetrable and supplied her with superhuman strength. I was with her when she received the news that doctors had run out of options for treating her illness. Her stoic response was that she didn't expect to hear that, followed by a request for an Arby's roast beef sandwich. You may have correctly deduced that food offered her as much solace as laughter, especially when chocolate was involved.

She also kept her hospice nurses in stitches, providing proof of a Kent State report published in the American Journal of Hospice and Palliative Care. The study revealed that humor was present in 85 percent of 132 observed nurse-based visits, which begs the question: If humor is a part of living, then why should it not be a part of dying?[62]

The saying that "laughter is the best medicine" is not just a quote. There are physiological benefits of laughter. It stimulates many organs with its intake of oxygen-rich air. It fires up and then cools down your stress response, resulting in the regulation of your heart rate and blood pressure. By providing circulation to your muscles, it can also reduce some of the physical symptoms of stress. Long-term effects include improving your immune system, acting as a natural painkiller, improving coping skills, and boosting your mood and self-esteem.[63] As for the aging process, the late, great Jimmy Buffet mused that "wrinkles will only go where the smiles have been."

Ecclesiastes 3:1-8 reminds us that there is a season for everything, including a time to laugh and a time to cry. When we muster a smile and turn that frown upside down, the ratio of hope to hopelessness can change proportionately. Mom and Aunt Martha lived the words of Proverbs 17:22: "*A joyful heart is a good medicine, but a crushed spirit dries up the bones.*" Their legacy of laughter permeated my soul, and I will be forever grateful for that.

---

[62] Mendoza, Ph.D., Marilyn. " The Healing Power of Laughter in Death and Grief." *Psychology Today,* 7 November 2016.

[63] Staff. "Stress Management." *Mayo Clinic,* 21 July 2021.

Compassionate Cooking

"Remember then that there is only one important time, and that time is now. The most important one is always the one you are with. And the most important thing to do is to do good for the one who is standing by your side."

The Three Questions by Jon J. Muth, adapted from a short story by Leo Tolstoy

A young boy, Nicolai, searches for answers to three questions: When is the best time to do things, who is the most important one, and what is the right thing to do? He fails to get satisfactory answers from his friends, the bird, the monkey, and the dog. But when he saves a panda and her baby, the old turtle, Leo, suggests that he found the answers to his questions. He was in the right place at the right time doing the most important thing.

We may ask ourselves the same questions, but the short answer is always to be kind. The Dalai Lama coined the phrase, "If you want others to be happy, practice compassion. If you want to be happy, practice compassion." I cannot think of a better way to do this than to cook for others.

Collecting cookbooks is a hobby of mine. My husband prefers the word hoarding, but he certainly does not complain when served a meal from my "hoarding" stash. While traveling, I'm always on the prowl for a book that features local flavors to add to my extensive collection. I devour these books voraciously, pardon the pun, as some read novels.

After my mother passed away, I was determined to preserve her recipe legacy along with those of other relatives. *Patricia's Potluck* includes perennial favorites, and this past Christmas, I made batches of some of my favorites, packaged them up, and gifted them to friends and family to serve as a reminder of the compassionate way Mom and other relatives showed their love through their cooking gifts. I hoped that these gifts would evoke memories of Christmas past in real time.

While teaching kindergarten, I had a precious child who asked her mom to bring a Poppy Seed Chicken Casserole to class because she wanted to share its deliciousness. And it was. It was comfort in a Pyrex dish with chunks of chicken swimming in pasta and a creamy sauce and topped with buttered Ritz cracker crumbs, and poppy seeds. Since that day, I have taken countless Poppy Seed Chicken Casseroles to families in need. Claire wanted to share something she loved with her friends, so, in a way, I am paying Claire's compassion forward.

To understand the word "compassion," we must look at the Latin root, *compait*, which means to "suffer with." The parable of the Good Samaritan exemplifies this. A man traveling from Jerusalem to Jericho was robbed, beaten, and left on the side of the road. A Samarian man came along and recognized that this man was in dire need of assistance. He gave him medical attention and took him to an inn to recuperate. Even today, we label people who go out of their way to bestow compassionate care to others as "Good Samaritans." These people fulfill the challenge of 1 Peter 3:8: "Finally, all of you, be like-minded, be sympathetic, love one another, be compassionate and humble."

Compassion fuels the twelfth step of the Alcoholics Anonymous program. Those who have reached this milestone are encouraged to "pay it forward" to others who are early in their recovery. This benefits the giver by diverting focus from self and the addiction and the receiver with support and encouragement. Without this step, the program would cease to exist.

The same can be said of cooking. We follow the steps of a recipe by buying the ingredients, prepping, assembling, and cooking. If that were the last step, the only one who would benefit is the cook. By sharing the fruits of our labor, we extend our gifts beyond our own homes, showing compassion to others. Sarah Ban Breathnach quotes her cookbook writer friend, Laurie Colwin: "I know that young children will wander away from the table, and that family life is never smooth, and that life itself is full, not only of charm, warmth, and comfort but of sorrow and tears. But whether we are happy or sad, we must be fed."[64]

---

[64] Breathnach, Sarah Ban. *Simple Abundance: A Daybook of Comfort and Joy,* New York City, Grand Central, 2009.

The Great Collaboration

"Your path will not be the same as the others. They will grow up to be warriors. Your path among the People will be remembered for a different reason."

The Legend of the Indian Paintbrush, retold and illustrated by Tomie dePaola

An Indian boy, Little Gopher, does not possess the strength to be a warrior. When his Dream Vision visits and assures him that he possesses artistic talents unique among his tribe, Little Gopher begins to paint scenes of hunts and other details of the reservation. But he is unable to recreate the sunset's vivid colors from the paints he produces from flowers and rocks, so he follows instructions from a voice in the night to take a pure white animal skin and go to the mountainside. There, he finds paintbrushes loaded with vibrant colors, and he quickly and accurately paints the sunset. His residual gift to the people occurs when the paintbrushes miraculously transform into flowers that multiply on the hillside and reemerge every year. From that moment on, he became known as He-Who-Brought-The-Sunset-To-The-Earth.

This is a story about recognizing one's talents and purpose in life. It also demonstrates how God directs us to use those gifts if we take the time and are willing to listen. A cautionary tale for mothers, it reminds us that our children are unique human beings with potential that our encouragement and support should mine. This is difficult when their plans are not aligned with ours and hard to witness when their choices seem to be directed by an absence of brain cells.

My oldest son, a thrill-seeking adrenaline junkie, spent much of his early years dirt-biking and participating in any activity that the coast had to offer. Horseback riding never once appeared on his radar until he and a friend signed up as horseback trail riding guides one summer in Jackson Hole. Seeking a quick fix for his equine inexperience, he summoned a friend to provide him with horseback riding-for-dummies lessons. This "friend" is now his wife. They presently own a 72-acre horse farm in Virginia. Go figure. It never crossed my mind when he was born that our mother-son dance at his wedding would be to *Mama*

Don't Let Your Babies Grow Up to be Cowboys (Waylon Jennings and Willie Nelson).

I never imagined my child growing up to be a cowboy, just like Jimmy Carter's mother never imagined that her son would one day be President of the United States. A former Navy man and peanut farmer who held the reins of the family farm after his daddy died, Jimmy's unassuming nature and Southern gentility certainly did not favorably feature him in such a role. His passion for improving the country's schools, housing, health care, and jobs provided the impetus for entering politics. But his term was riddled with inflation and high interest rates, gas shortages, and an Iranian hostage crisis, and pundits painted him as an ineffective president. But his achievements outside of the office are his enduring legacy. Traveling to dangerous and impoverished parts of the world to promote peace and prevent bloodshed earned him a Nobel Peace Prize. He swung a hammer with expertise to provide housing for those in need with Habitat for Humanity. But in everything he did, he called upon God to guide him and praised Him for the opportunities to help others, including his numerous years of teaching Sunday School.

At kindergarten graduation, every year, my class sang *I Am a Promise,* written by Gloria Gaither. Adorably sung by a group of fidgety five-year-olds who were undoubtedly clueless as to the depth of meaning of the lyrics, the song asserts, "I am a promise, a possibility, I am a promise, with a capital P. I am a great big bundle of potentiality."

The song goes on to say, "I am learning to hear God's voice, and I am trying to make the right choices." Sarah Ban Breathnach titles this joint effort with God "The Great Collaboration." She speaks to our unwillingness to explore and share our talents because we don't feel they are adequate for the task. But she cites many artists, including the author of *Uncle Tom's Cabin* and *Madame Butterfly* composer Giacomo Puccini, who claim to be simply instruments of God.

God doesn't want us to hide the gifts and talents He has bestowed on us. He wants us to shake off the mantle of self-doubt and create with abandon. Ban Breathnach explains that the "world needs your gift as much as you need to bestow it."[65] He wants us to take creative risks.

In Matthew 25:14-30, a man gathered his three servants before going on a trip and gave them bags of silver. While he was gone, two of

---

[65] Breathnach, Sarah Ban. *Simple Abundance: A Daybook of Comfort and Joy,* New York City, Grand Central, 2009.

the men invested their windfall and doubled their original investment. The third man buried his silver in the ground. Upon his return, the owner praised the two who invested and scorned the man who did not. The man who played it safe made the riskiest choice because he squandered the opportunity to grow his investment. He was unwilling to take a creative risk. The takeaway from this story is explained in Matthew 25:29: "For whoever has will be given more, and they will have an abundance. Whoever does not have, even what they have will be taken from them."

There is a saying that "Some people make the world a better place just by being in it." Jimmy Carter is one of those people. We should all aspire to be remembered this way. But to do so, we must give back, seek a better world, and, most of all, take those risks that God wants us to take. He gave us talents, and we must use them.

Life: The Great Balancing Act

"So be sure when you step with care and great tact. And remember that life's A Great Balancing Act."

The Places You'll Go by Dr. Seuss

Dr. Seuss addresses the Great Balancing Act of Life with humor, rollicking rhymes, and whimsical illustrations. In just fifty-six pages, he imparts a lifetime of wisdom. He acknowledges all the facets of life that make us who we are, including failure and loss.

As a kindergarten teacher, I signed countless copies of this book. Five is such a hopeful age, a life beckoning with opportunities instead of a past filled with squandered chances and regrets. These innocent, eternal optimists approach life with abandon, harboring no thoughts of moderation, prioritizing, or balancing. It is the aging process that catapults us into a world where we struggle to maintain an equilibrium between the forces of good and evil.

My oldest son came home from elementary school one day and triumphantly announced that he and a friend had signed up for the school's talent show. As my brain frantically scanned its hard drive for the "talent" to which he referred, he proudly clarified it for me: He and his friend planned to "bongo board.*"* It took everything in my power not to laugh out loud.

To enlighten you, a bongo board looks like a skateboard, but instead of wheels, the platform rests on a cylindrical roller. The "rider" stands on the platform with feet placed on either side of the roller. The purpose is to balance on it without letting either end touch the ground. This "talent" would be performed to the song All-Star by Smash Mouth. If you've never heard that song, here's a snippet:

"Somebody once told me the world is gonna roll me I ain't the sharpest tool in the shed
She was looking kind of dumb with her finger and her thumb in the shape of an "L" on her forehead."

At least their music selection was on point.

The night of the show arrived. We sat by the door to make a quick exit. By the time they performed their great balancing act, I was convinced that I had judged them too harshly. They had simply confused talent with egotism.

Life and bongo boards have a lot in common. We constantly straddle the fulcrum of hindsight and foresight, potential and lost opportunities, optimism and pessimism. Finding ourselves teetering and tottering between making appropriate choices, we are often guided more by our mindset than our mindfulness. The possibilities and potential of our "board" are stifled by the "fulcrum" of our attitudes.

Most often, the impediment to leading a balanced life is time. There never seems to be enough. Juggling the demands of jobs, family, and other pursuits, decisions are made on the fly with little thought of repercussions. Knee-jerk reactions fueled by emotions seldom yield sound outcomes.

In her book *By Way of Grace*, Paula Huston explains that temperance holds the key to balance for Christians. Often misconstrued as "unhealthy denials of life's pleasures," the true definition of temperance refers to keeping "our passions in check" due to our deeply instilled spiritual principles. She relates to St. Ignatius, who spoke of people with "disordered affections," people whose decisions are guided by pleasure and not wisdom.[66] A temperate person taps into her God-given desires and passions but does not allow them to take control and hijack her choices.

Despite times when Jesus found himself amid turmoil, with people clamoring for his attention, he found a way to temper his priorities by turning to God in prayer. Awaiting his crucifixion, he sought peace with his destiny through prayer in the Garden of Gethsemane. He found balance by not giving into the insistent demands of the world but by biding his time in the presence of his Father.

Ironically, this one-click, tech-efficient world in which we live streamlines our lives to free up more time, but we still find ourselves teetering precariously on our bongo boards, racing against the clock to stay balanced. We often insist we don't have the time, but we must take the time to sit in God's presence to achieve spiritual equilibrium.

---

[66] Huston, Paula. "By Way of Grace: Moving from Faithfulness to Holiness." Chicago, IL, Loyola Press, 2007.

121

Matthew 11:28-30 reminds us to take His yoke so he can give rest to those who are "weary and burdened."

I have always told my children that life is a journey, not a destination, especially when that journey is precarious. As uneven and inconsistent as the course may be, soulful symmetry is achievable through trust and faith. And then, Smash Mouth, the world won't roll you.

THE GREAT BALANCING ACT

Forgive and Forget,
No Revenge nor Regret

"On the way home, Lilly opened her purse. Her glasses and coins were inside. And so was a note from Mr. Slinger. It said: Today was a difficult day. Tomorrow will be better."

Lilly's Purple Plastic Purse by Kevin Henkes

In this book, Kevin Henkes imparts a lesson about the power of forgiveness. When Lilly brings her purse, movie star glasses, and shiny quarters to school and interrupts her teacher's lesson, Mr. Slinger takes them away until the end of the day. Lilly retaliates by writing an angry note to him. He responds with a note of his own, attributing her hostility to a difficult day and announcing that he holds no grudge. Instead of punishing Lilly, he uses the situation to model forgiveness.

In the research article "Bad is Stronger than Good," the authors proclaim that "bad emotions, bad parents, and bad feedback have a greater impact than good ones, and bad information is processed more thoroughly than good." These authors also report that it takes five positive experiences to negate one bad one.[67] I could not agree more. Retail experiences fueled by grouchy, unmotivated, or phone-obsessed customer service representatives contribute larger deposits to my memory bank than pleasant ones. Yelp is my retaliatory superpower, and I am not afraid to use it.

Technology has expedited our responses to indignities and irritations. The instant gratification of emails and texts has replaced cooling-off periods afforded by letter writing. Undoing these missives is akin to unscrambling an egg. Trust me, I've tried. My knee-jerk reactions punch my ticket to Regretville every single time. It might behoove me to tattoo the quote "Taste your words before you serve" on my forehead.

The parable of the prodigal son demonstrates the healing power of forgiveness. When the younger of two sons asked for his share of his inheritance, the father obliged. The son lived high on the hog until he

---

[67] Baumeister, Roy F., et. al. "Bad is Stronger Than Good." *University of Minnesota Twin Cities,* 16 April 2001.

squandered every dime. He found himself working on a farm, eating the same food he fed the pigs. In desperation, he returned home and asked his father to take him back. Instead of reprimanding him for his foolishness, the father welcomed him with open arms, gave him a ring, and threw a party in his honor. (Luke 15:11-32)

Witnessing this lavish celebration, the other son became irate, but his father explained that the son whom he had assumed was dead and returned alive brought him relief and joy. He chose to forgive and forget, not revenge nor regret.

In 2015, Dylan Roof walked into a Bible study at the AME Emmanuel Church in Charleston. After being warmly greeted, he worshipped with the twelve attendees over the next hour. But in an act of racial terrorism, he shot nine of them to death. At his bond hearing, relatives of the victims stood up one by one, offering forgiveness to the man accused of murdering their beloved family members. This cold-blooded attack by a white supremacist with the intention of provoking a race war was a significant event in the Black Lives Matter movement, a time when violent deaths of African Americans were triggering protests and rioting throughout the nation. But rather than declaring hatred for this man whose skin color did not match their own, instead of spouting a litany of indignities and demanding justice, the relatives offered forgiveness. Instead of being engulfed in a race war, Charleston erupted in grace, led by the people most affected by this massacre.

These Charlestonians exhibited the "unoffendable hearts of Jesus." As author Joanna Weaver points out, giving hearts don't wait for an offender's repentance to bestow mercy but instead follow the reminder of Colossians 3:13: "Make allowances for each other's faults and forgive anyone who offends you. Remember, the Lord forgave you, so you must forgive others."[68]

Like the prodigal son, our children may make choices that do not reflect the values we have worked hard to instill, doing something so grievous as to endanger themselves or others. The pain Roof's parents felt upon learning that their child was responsible for this atrocious act is unimaginable. While we don't always like the choices our children make and, hopefully, we will never experience anything to this extreme, how we react will forever alter the relationship. Forgiveness is a bitter pill to swallow, especially when the hurt cuts

---

[68] Weaver, Joanna. "Embracing Trust." Grand Rapids, MI, Revell Books, 2022.

deep. But the longer the wound festers, the formation of scar tissue threatens to serve as a permanent reminder of the pain it conceals.

However, it is essential to note that forgiveness and acceptance can be mutually exclusive. Forgiveness is a matter of the heart, a compassionate willingness to release someone from shame. Acceptance implies approval. We can forgive destructive behaviors without putting a big red bow on them. Natural consequences unburden us from the responsibility of addressing punishment for their decisions.

In his book *Forgiveness*, Tim Keller reminds us that the "heart of forgiveness is release."[69] By the sacrifice of Jesus' death on the cross, we are assured forgiveness and release from our sins. When we face the conundrum of releasing or holding hostage our anger and resentment, it helps to heed the words of Bernard Meltzer, "when you forgive, you in no way change the past - but you sure do change the future." We can stay mired in vindictiveness and divisiveness or choose forgiveness and unity.

Mr. Slinger taught Lilly the concrete and calculable subjects of "reading, writing, and 'rithmetic." But his gracious and lasting lesson of forgiveness made an indelible impression on her life—just like that tattoo I may get one day.

FLAG DESIGNED BY GIL SHULER

---

[69] Keller, Tim. "Forgive: Why Should I and How Can I?" New York City, Viking Books, 2022.

The Perennial Love of a Mother's Heart

"I'll love you forever, I'll like you for always, as long as you're living, my baby you'll be."

Love You Forever by Robert Munsch

This refrain reverberates throughout the seasons of a mother raising her son, even when he assumes the responsibility of caring for her in her old age.

This reminds me of an old saying that, paraphrased, frames the timeline of motherhood as short-lived on the hand-holding segment but eternally heart-filling. Our wombs provide homes for nine months, but our hearts hold space forever. The tireless attention to our children's wants and needs, ambitions and heartaches, successes and failures shape them but also redefine who we are in the process. They don't become ours; we become theirs.

Cultivating a garden is not unlike mothering. We hope for perennials, the established species that promise to return yearly. They are the stalwarts, the dependable ones, living the lives we dreamed for them.

But the annuals, the one-season wonders, provide variety and character to the garden. They tend to be like most children. Varying in color from bright to subdued, some bloom abundantly, while others open sporadically. Some grow upright, established by their root placement. Others spread out freely, untethered by root support. Constant watering, pinching off dead blooms, and pampering are necessary for some, while others thrive despite their circumstances. Annuals don't usually come back year after year, but sometimes they do, depending on the complications and severity of the seasons. And when they do surface after enduring especially difficult conditions, they bloom more impactfully and beautifully, watered and fed by the hardships.

Face it. As much as we love our children, they can be our most profound joy yet our greatest challenge. It's sticky, messy, dirty, heart-wrenching, and time-sucking. Our days are filled with carpools and catastrophes, and we ride the struggle bus of schedule equilibrium when choosing between our lives and theirs. The girl's night we missed because a child had a fever. The vacation we canceled to attend a sporting event. The time taken off from work to meet with the principal about a child's misbehavior. The agonizing heartache endured due to a child's wayward path. "To have a child is momentous. It is to decide to have your heart go walking around outside your body."[70] Those hearts are the vessels that hold every ounce of our delights and despair.

But this selfless devotion also fuels our incredible strength, the ability to recognize our children's gifts amidst the messes of their lives, to abandon control, and to allow God to channel those talents and even their poor choices according to His will. Some of the strongest mothers I know belong to a support group that I attend weekly. Whether we "gave birth to, adopted, fostered, or have a child who shines from above," we share the common bond of a mother's heart. There is not one situation that He cannot use for the greater good, but we must understand that our role is partner, not sole proprietor. My mom never questioned this.

For the third year in a row, I cannot call her to wish her a happy Mother's Day, and my heart aches for her every single day. As I navigate my motherhood journey, I understand the sacrifices she made while raising my two brothers and me. I know her joy in watching children grow and flourish. I also admit to the same helplessness when tasked with helping my children through challenging times that she must have felt while dealing with my youngest brother's bipolar disorder. But I will never comprehend her ability to move forward after his suicide.

But then again, maybe I do. Being a mother is "learning about strengths you didn't know you had…and dealing with fears you didn't know existed." (Linda Wooten) My mother found that strength through trusting her Lord and Savior. Her faith moved the mountains of doubt as to why Brock was called to his heavenly home at the tender age of forty-two. She understood that his age was insignificant to God's will. My mother was many things…kind, stoic, funny, and messy (which drove me crazy) …but her enduring gift to me was faith. We often kidded her about her obsession with her iPad and her social media stalking, but her most faithful dependence was on her ever-present Bible. She read it, and she lived it.

---

[70] Stone, Elizabeth." Making the Decision to Have a Child is Momentous." *Human Coalition,* 16 September 2023.

Most often read at weddings to guide young couples in their commitment to one another, Corinthians 13:4-6 also correlates beautifully with a mother's love. "Love is patient, love is kind. It does not envy, it does not boast, it is not proud. It does not dishonor others, it is not self-seeking, it is not easily angered, it keeps no record of wrongs." My mother embodied every single one of these characteristics with grace. She tended her gardens, her children, and grandchildren with unwavering patience and devotion. We bloomed under her care, and I will love her forever for that.

FAITH
Planting Seeds of Faith

"People come from far and near to look at this flower. It is the tallest flower they have ever seen. It is a giant flower".

The Tiny Seed by Eric Carle

One Autumn, a group of seeds blown by the wind begins a year-long journey of survival through seasonal obstacles. Only one, the tiniest of the bunch, finds purchase in a fertile place and grows into a beautiful flower. Some would argue that this seed just got lucky. Others might counter that it was the enormous faith encased within its tiny shell that propelled it to its final destination.

We live on a creek with a dock. During the summers, my children used to revel in jumping off the roof at high tide. They are now grown, but they recently visited with friends in tow. Recreating their childhood pastime, I watched as, one by one, they took the leap of faith and hurled themselves into the water. All except one. This young man stood on that roof for the longest time as my children and their cohorts encouraged him to jump. Nothing could convince him. Not that I blame him one bit. I certainly would not haul my sixty- something-year-old self into the water of questionable depth and teeming with critters. I am years removed from my stupid college days.

Faith. A word that conveys confidence and assurance. It is "taking the first step when you don't see the whole staircase." (Martin Luther King Jr.) When Jesus' friends asked Him how they could strengthen their faith, he replied, "Truly I tell you, if you have faith as small as a mustard seed, you can say to this mountain, 'Move from here to there,' and it will move. Nothing will be impossible for you." (Matthew 17:20)

It is easy to see why Jesus chose the mustard seed analogy. The mustard seed can grow in rocky or sandy soil, just as a small amount of faith can sustain us during unstable times. Pruning the mustard bush encourages growth in the same way discarding the unmanageable aspects of our lives can lead to healthier and more robust existences. The plant leaves produce mustard for our hot dogs, and the seeds provide numerous health and medicinal benefits. Our faith strengthens us by feeding our spiritual health and empowering us to face life's challenges.

Among the many inspiring stories in the Bible, Shadrach, Meshach, and Abednego are the standard bearers in the face of adversity. King Nebuchadnezzar commanded the creation of a golden statue and ordered everyone to bow down and worship it. When these three men refused to obey, the King had them thrown into a fiery furnace at temperatures seven times higher than usual. Yet, when the furnace was opened the next day, the three men were unharmed and accompanied by an angel sent by God to protect them. Stunned by what he saw, the King reversed his commandment to bow to his idol and demanded that his people worship the God of Shadrach, Meshach, and Abednego. (Daniel 3)

As Terry Tempest Williams beautifully puts it, "Faith is the centerpiece of a connected life. It allows us to live by the grace of invisible strands. It is a belief in wisdom superior to our own. Faith becomes a teacher in the absence of fact." The stories of Shadrach, Meshach, Abednego, David, and Daniel are powerful examples of how faith, when unwavering, can protect and empower us. These men faced seemingly insurmountable challenges, yet their faith was their force shield, providing security and protection.

We will most likely never confront a giant or enter a lion's den. But we may be challenged to endure the heat of an explosive situation or take a leap of faith into the unknown, especially when it comes to our children. We can rise to the task when we are rooted with just a tiny seed of invisible but unshakeable faith. Be assured by these words from Hebrews 11:1: "Now faith is the assurance of things hoped for, the conviction of things not seen."

Maybe in life, but I'm still not jumping off the dock.

Hope is a Four-Letter Word

"Then he nibbled a hole in the cocoon, pushed his way out, and he was a beautiful butterfly."

The Very Hungry Caterpillar by Eric Carle

In this beloved children's book, we follow the life cycle of a butterfly, written and illustrated in true Carle collage style. There is no better example of hope than the metamorphosis from a simple egg to an intricately God-designed creation.

At my weekly moms' support group meeting, we gather to share, commiserate, cry, and often laugh about the absurdity of our children's antics. Sometimes, the only way to adequately describe our feelings is with a four-letter word. At times, we even regard "hope" as one of those vulgarities. Whether a situation is beyond hope, or we have given up, hope feels out of our reach.

We often use this word to express our desires or dreams. I "hope" I get that job. I "hope" it doesn't rain today. I "hope" I'm (or not) pregnant. I "hope" my child will recover from his illness. Hoping will never guarantee the job, the weather, the pregnancy, or the recovery. The only real hope we have is in God's sovereign plan for our lives.

An article on PsychCentral.com cites seven types of hope: Inborn, Chosen, Bargainers, Borrowed, Unrealistic, False, and Mature. When our children suffer from an illness, whether it is uninvited or self-inflicted, we often respond with Unrealistic (they will miraculously recover) or False (we will be okay if they get better) Hope. But Mature Hope is realistic hope. This is the hope that is based on something other than outcomes. "Mature hope is based on meaning. In other words, things are worthwhile regardless of how they turn out."[71]

The acacia tree provides a great analogy for hope. Grown in the dry riverbeds of the Judean desert as well as the deserts of Nevada and Arizona, its uses are plentiful. It provides shade and firewood, camels eat their leaves, and the Bedouins boil the sap to use as medicine for scrapes and stomach troubles. Its roots grow

---

[71] Borchard, Theresa. "The Seven Kinds of Hope." *Psych Central, 10 December 2009.*

in harsh conditions and tap into water sources that other plants cannot reach. Its slow growth results in wood that is hard and dense, resistant to water and insect damage, making it the perfect material for the construction of the Ark of the Covenant.[72] Its uses…shade, warmth, healing, sustenance, and protection…mirror God's promises. It is in the shade of His protection that we receive sustenance for the growth and healing of emotional wounds. When we are firmly rooted in the security of God's promise never to abandon us, the water of life flows abundantly and frequently.

Like the acacia tree, which draws strength from God's love to endure the heat and drought of difficult times, we, too, can find reassurance and stability in our faith during our challenges. As Jeremiah 17:7-8 reminds us: "For he shall be like a tree planted by the waters, which spreads out its roots by the river and will not fear when heat comes; but its leaf will be green and will not be anxious in the year of drought, nor will cease from yielding fruit."

It is tempting to express hope as a word teeming with uncertainty. However, God wants us to trust in the biblical meaning of hope and be confident in our expectations and desires for the future, but not in the certainty of a particular outcome. This mature hope fosters spiritual dependence and releases us from false and unrealistic outlooks. As the author, Lysa Terkeurst, defines hope and hopelessness: "If I am letting a mess define me, I will feel hopeless. If I am letting a mess refine me, I will be hopeful." This is a reminder that it is not adversity that shapes one's character but the reaction to it. When we respond with biblical hope, the potential vulgarity of this four-letter word is replaced with promise. And that promise is found in Romans 15:13: "May the God of hope fill you with all joy and peace in believing, so that by the power of the Holy Spirit you may abound in hope."

The next time you see a butterfly, be reminded of that hope.

---

[72] Cushman, Nancy. *Lessons from the Acacia Tree.* Desert Southwest Conference: The United Methodist Church, 1 October 2019.

Peace Like a River

"Mrs. Large ran a deep, hot bath. She emptied half a bottle of bath foam in the water, plonked on her bath hat, and got in. She poured herself a cup of tea and lay back with her eyes closed. It was heaven."

Five Minutes Peace by Jill Murphy

Mrs. Large was enjoying five minutes of peace. Until she wasn't. Her children came in one by one to play the flute, read a book to her, and dump toys in the tub. Then the children jumped in, and she jumped out and was able to find three minutes and forty-five seconds in the kitchen before they found her again.

Finding peace is not unlike taking an uninterrupted bath. Soaking in a tub filled with warm water and fragrant bath beads, languishing in that aromatic cocoon relaxes the body, quiets the mind, and soothes the soul. But emerging from its tranquility abruptly awakens the system. Life is like that. Just when we find ourselves cruising in our comfort zones, a reality check hijacks our sense of complacency.

I am the poster child for what not to do when life takes an unexpected detour. As a psychotic perfectionist and master manipulator, diversion from my well-crafted plans kicks my kneejerk mentality into overdrive. My lack of patience in these situations drives immediate solutions, often lacking in forethought and common sense. The results become offerings on my altar of peace.

Let's face it: This world is a mess. It is rife with wars, racial divisions, clashes over gender status, battles over abortion rights, political corruption, poverty and homelessness, and post-pandemic aftershocks. And if these external conflicts are not enough, internal struggles caused by fear, uncertainty, anxiety, depression, addiction, mental illness, and grief complicate matters even more. Some days, it is a wonder that we even make it out of bed.

The 1960s Vietnam-era antiwar crusade is known as the longest-sustained protest movement in the history of the United States. In 1967, "The Summer of Love" bore witness to 100,000 people gathered in San Francisco to promote peace and love and protest the war. Ironically, what began as a peaceful objection in the form of

133

marches, sit-ins, and picket demonstrations turned into angry confrontations, most notably the killings at Kent State. In 1970, the National Guard fired into a student protest, killing four and injuring nine. This "peaceful protest" became anything but that.[73]

Finding peace amidst the chaos is challenging. As Paul reminds us, "If possible, so far as it depends on you, live peaceably with all." (Romans 12:18). Note that Paul refers to "you," not "them." Choices made by other people will wreak havoc if you let them. As the saying goes, "Poor planning on your part does not constitute an emergency on my part." There is no better example of this than children and their last-minute requests for cupcakes or project materials. Talk about peace suckers. To maintain harmony and avoid major meltdowns, we acquiesce and find ourselves rambling around Walmart at all hours of the morning in search of poster boards and puffy paint.

However, project materials pale in comparison to the issues we face with teenagers and young adults. Walmart all-nighters don't hold a candle to frantic middle-of-the-night calls. The peace of uninterrupted, deep sleep dissipates in a skinny second at the sound of that ring. Those REM dreams quickly transform into real-life nightmares.

Jesus talked with his disciples shortly before His crucifixion. He knew they were fearful, but he comforted them by promising this: "Peace I leave with you; my peace I give you. I do not give to you as the world gives. Do not let your hearts be troubled, and do not be afraid." (John 14:27-31) He did not promise them easy lives, void of conflict or fear. Instead, he assured them they would live together in peace when He returned, granting them a sense of genuine tranquility instead of conditional serenity. This serves as a reminder that when we abandon our dependence on situational peace and replace it with spiritual calm, we, too, can rest in the peace that only God can provide.

The song, *When Peace, Like a River,* compares a body of water to peace that continually flows despite the obstacles and disappointments in our lives. The author, Horatio Safford, was well qualified to pen this beloved hymn. His four daughters perished   when the English sailing vessel they were aboard capsized in 1873. He learned of this tragedy with a note from his wife stating simply "saved alone. " The song's lyrics lament Safford's sorrows and trials, but the chorus repeatedly reassures that "all is well with my soul."[74]

---

[73] Kent State Shootings." *www.history.com*, 4 May 2023.

[74] "Hymn Histories/When Peace Like a River." *Lifeway Women*. 3 August 2022.

"Life with God is not immunity from difficulties, but peace in difficulties." (C. S. Lewis) Peace is a gift from God, the gift of our partnership with Him. Regardless of any situation, this relationship allows our souls to be well.

Hamlin Creek, Isle of Palms

The Amazing Gift of Grace

"Grace cheered up; then she remembered something else. "Natalie said I can't be Peter Pan because I'm black," she said. Ma looked angry. But before she could speak, Nana said, "It seems like Natalie is another one that don't know nothing. You can be anything you want, Grace, if you put your mind to it."

Amazing Grace by Mary Hoffman

The name Grace is derived from the Latin root *gratia*, meaning "favor" or "blessing." Being a Black girl does not deter Grace from trying out for the role of Peter Pan, generally played by a white boy. Her hard work and polite determination find "favor" in the eyes of the director, and she is "blessed" with the title role. Grace is aptly named.

Grace forms the backbone of the Christian faith. The character Grace earns hers, but spiritual grace is bestowed freely if we believe in and live Christian lives, regardless of the mistakes we make. As Tim Keller reminds us, "We need to remember that we are saved by grace when we fail. But we need to remember it much more when we succeed." We are covered by a blanket of benevolence no matter what we do.

My Aunt Martha exuded grace. When she was diagnosed thirteen years ago with ALS, she was given three years to live. Our family believes her longevity stems from her promise to her mother, my grandmother, that she would take care of my mother. My mother was the eldest of the two, but my grandmother's maternal intuition must have alerted her that my mother would face challenges requiring her sister's support. And she was not wrong.

As her favorite, albeit only, niece, I have always regarded her as "another mother." Over the last thirteen years, I watched her decline but never witnessed self-pity. Throughout the trials and tribulations of her life, I never once heard her bad mouth, demean, or cuss. A visiting neighbor once asked if she could bring her anything. Her reply? "I have everything I need." An amazing statement from a woman who was bedridden and could no longer feed herself or tend to her basic needs. The world lost this beautiful human being on July 16, 2023.

Victor Frankl was a psychologist who survived the Holocaust and used his experiences in his therapy to help people with their sufferings. He determined that hope was the common denominator of those who survived their dire circumstances. This led Frankl to surmise that "life only has meaning in any circumstance if we have a hope that suffering, circumstance, or even death cannot destroy."[75] During the years she suffered from this wretched disease, her body in constant decline, Aunt Martha clung to hope. Not "the feeling of expectation and desire for a certain thing to happen," as the dictionary defines it, but Biblical hope. The words of 2 Corinthians 12:9-10 provided her with strength: "My grace is sufficient for you, for my power is made perfect in weakness." His grace sustained and strengthened her daily.

The beloved hymn *Amazing Grace* was written by John Newton, a coarse and unlikeable man. Newton ran away from home in his teens to become a sailor and, subsequently, a slave trader, a distasteful and unscrupulous occupation. But when he nearly died in a shipwreck, he prayed earnestly for salvation from the storm. As the storm subsided, overcome with emotion, he decided to abandon his life of debauchery and embrace Christianity. Newton transitioned from a drunken slave captain to a Christian priest and, ultimately, an abolitionist of slavery. His lived experiences provided the lyrics for this song of redemption from his wicked life.

"Amazing grace, how sweet the sound that saved a wretch like me! I once was lost, but now I'm found. I was blind, but now I see."

Newton unwittingly penned the theme song for those who have lost their way and turned to God for forgiveness and mercy. In her book, *Mostly What God Does,* Savannah Guthrie explains grace this way: "God does not wait for perfection before he forgives us. He does not require a changed life before he shows us mercy. His mercy precedes us."[76]

This promise is especially comforting when our children stray from the paths of righteousness. No matter the depth or breadth of their betrayals, God extends the olive branch of grace and lovingly gathers them in and grants them mercy. When they relinquish their agendas in

[75] Muldoon, Tim. "Facing our hardships with hope: lessons from Victor Frankl." *Medium,* 28 March 2020.

[76] Guthrie, Savannah. "Mostly What God Does." Nashville, TN, W Publishing, 2024.

exchange for God's mercy, "their chains are gone; they've been set free."

As Sarah Ban Breathnach reminds us, "Grace is available for each of us every day—our spiritual daily bread—but we've got to remember to ask for it with a grateful heart and try not to worry about whether there will be enough for tomorrow. There will be."[77]

[77] Breathnach, Sarah Ban. "Something More: Excavating Your Authentic Self." New York City, Warner Books, 1998.

Trust Comes in All Sizes

"Big lion. Big net. Big, big trouble."

The Lion and the Mouse by Jerry Pinkney

This book retells one of Aesop's fables about a mighty lion who catches a mouse. The mouse begs the lion to free him in exchange for returning the favor one day. When the lion becomes trapped in a net, the mouse chews through to free him. The lion trusted that the mouse would stay true to his promise, and the lion's life was spared.

My yellow lab, Lady, is the most loyal and trusting dog on earth. We walk the beach most mornings, unleashed, because I trust her not to wander too far, and she trusts me to be on the watch should her sand-sniffing ADHD kick in. She also knows without a doubt that Ms. Karen will have treats.

One day, as we began our trek back to the path leading us home, Lady suddenly bolted back down to the beach. Out of fear-certainly not because a run was high on my agenda--I took after her, quickly losing sight. (It should be noted that a 5-year-old Lab and a sixty-something-year-old woman are not exactly well matched in the sprinting department.) About two blocks later, I got close enough to see that she had stopped and was patiently waiting for a treat from Ms. Karen.

Trust is tricky. The lion warily trusted the mouse. Lady unconditionally trusted Ms. Karen to have a treat. Peter was able to walk on water because he trusted Jesus. Until he didn't. When he turned his eyes away, he began to sink. He cried out for Jesus to save Him, to which He reached out his hand and replied, "You of little faith," he said, "Why did you doubt?" (Matthew 13:31)

In a variety of contexts, the Bible tells us 365 times not to fear, but Peter's fear created a chasm between his situation and his unconditional trust in Jesus. As Lysa Terkeurst explains, God wants us to rest, not resist, by trusting Him. The difference between these two words is the letter "I." It's our self-reliance that prevents us from relying on Him. We resist trusting when waiting takes too long. We resist trusting when we run out of options. We resist trusting when we do not like the answer. We will only find *anapauo* rest…fresh hope…when we stop resisting and start resting.[78]

Another problem with trust is the ease with which it breaks and the difficulty of rebuilding it. Relationships with our children are a house of cards that we construct over a lifetime but topple quickly when we are dealt a hand of deceitful and hurtful behaviors. Like the lion to the mouse, some situations appear too large and unsurmountable to ever recover that trust. However, like Peter, when we allow Jesus to walk with us during the reconstruction, it is possible to rebuild. It may take a long time to cross the river of doubt, but it can happen.

I saved the topic of trust as the last chapter of this book because, above all others, it is where our ultimate strength for overcoming life's challenges lies. In Chapter One, we acknowledge the pain of unanswered prayers. It is through trust that we find those answers.

As a mother in recovery from self-reliance, I have walked through fires with my children. My feet are burned and blistered because they were shod in shoes of autonomy. It has taken time and many relapses, but I finally realize that their own feet will carry them in the direction God provides. My newfound trust allows me to walk barefoot through the fields of motherhood and breathe freedom from control. I can rest.

---

[78] Terkeurst, Lysa. "Embraced." Nashville, TN: Harper Collins, 2019.

EPILOGUE

This book serves as a personal reminder that there is always hope. I have tasted both the sweetness and the bitterness of motherhood, but like a balanced diet energizes my body, the confluence of these experiences has enriched my spiritual health.

In my Mothers Gathering support group, we share our lived experiences but do not judge or advise. *Grace from Grit* was written with the same intent. Motherhood is the hardest job you will ever love, and if anyone walks away with an insight, an "aha" moment, because of my journey, I have done my job as a writer.

From one mother's heart to another, I wish you well.

CHAPTER	BOOK
1	Twain, Mark. *Huckleberry Finn*. London: New York City: Charles L. Webster & Co, February 18, 1885.
2	Henkes, Kevin. *Wemberly Worried*. New York City: Greenwillow Books, April 27, 2010.
3	Green, Andi. *The Very Frustrated Monster*. New York City: Monsters in My Head, October 25, 2012.
4	Carle, Eric. *The Mixed-Up Chameleon*.
5	Demi. *The Empty Pot*. New York City: Square Fish, September 15, 1996.
6	Milne, A. A. *Winnie the Pooh*. London: Methuen & Co. and New York City: E. P. Dutton, October 14, 1926.
7	Curtis, Jamie Lee (author), Cornell, Laura (illustrator). *Today I Feel Silly and Other Moods*. New York City: Harper Collins, July 1, 1998.
8	O'Neill, Alexis (author), Huliska-Beith, Laura (illustrator. *Mean Jean, the Recess Queen*. New York City: Scholastic, February 1, 2002.
9	Spires, Ashley. *The Most Magnificent Thing*. Toronto: Kids Can Press, April 11, 2014.
10	Bang, Molly. *When Sophie Gets Angry—Really, Really Angry*. New York City: Scholastic, June 1, 2004.
11	Dr. Seuss. *Horton Hatches the Egg*. New York City: Random House, 1940.
12	Polacco, Patricia. *Thunder Cake*. London: Puffin, August 25, 1997.
13	Holmes, Margaret (author), Pillo, Cary (illustrator). *A Terrible Thing Happened*. Maumee, OH: Imagination Press, February 15, 2020.
14	Cain, Janan. *The Way I Feel*. Seattle, WA: Parenting Press, March 2, 2021.
15	Wilhelm, Hans. *I'll Always Love You*. Decorah, IA: Dragonfly Books, December 12, 1988.
16	Curtis, Jamie Lee (author), Cornell, Laura (illustrator). *My Brave Year of Firsts: Tries, Sighs, and High-Fives*. New York City: Harper Collins, December 4, 2012.
17	Finison, Carrie (author), Wiseman, Daniel (illustrator). *Don't Hug Doug: (He Doesn't Like It)*. New York City: G. P. Putman's Sons Books for Young Readers, January 26, 2021.
18	Ippen, Chandra Gosh (author), Ippen Jr., Erich. *You Weren't with Me*. San Francisco, CA: Piplo Productions. February 12, 2019/
19	Martin, Emily Winfield. *The Wonderful Things You Will Be*. New York City: Random House Books for Young Readers, August 25, 2015.
20	Carle, Eric. *A House for Hermit Crab*. New York City: Simon and Schuster, 1987
21	Henkes, Kevin. *Waiting*. New York City: Greenwillow, September 1, 2015.

22	Henkes, Kevin. *Owen.* New York City: Greenwillow, September 15, 1993.
23	Boelts, Maribeth (author), Jones, Noah Z. (illustrator). *Those Shoes.* Somerville, MA: Candlewick Press, June 9, 2009.
24	Editors. *The Lion King (Disney Scripted Classic).* San Diego: CA, April 5, 2022.
25	Feinberg, Heather Hawk (author), Kellogg, Chamisa (illustrator). *Crying is Like the Rain: A Story of Mindfulness and Feelings.* Ann Arbor, MI: Tilbury House, September 15, 2020.
26	Silverstein, Shel. *The Giving Tree.* New York City: Harper and Row, January 1, 1964.
27	Dr. Seuss. *What Pet Should I Get?* New York City: Random House, July 28, 2015.
28	Curtis, Jamie Lee (author), Cornell, Laura (illustrator). *It's Hard to Be Five: Learning How to Work My Control Panel.* New York City: Harper Collins, July 31, 2007.
29	Henkes, Kevin. *Chrysanthemum.* New York City: Greenwillow, September 15, 1993.
30	Dr. Seuss. *Yertle the Turtle.* New York City: Random House, April 12, 1958.
31	Curtis, Jamie Lee (author), Cornell, Laura (illustrator). *I'm Gonna Like Me: Letting Off a Little Self-Esteem.* New York City: Harper Collins, January 1, 2002.
32	Berenstain, Jan and Stan. *The Berenstain Bears Count Their Blessings.* New York
	City: Random House for Young Readers, October 24, 1995.
33	Stevens, Janet. *Tops and Bottoms.* San Diego, CA: Harcourt Brace, March 29, 1995.
34	Wood, Douglas (author), Chee, Cheng-Kee. *Old Turtle.* New York City: Scholastic, March 1, 2007.
35	Muth, Jon J. *Zen Shorts.* New York City: Scholastic, March 1, 2005.
36	Falconer, Ian. *Olivia Dances for Joy.* New York City: Atheneum Books for Young Readers, October 27, 2009.
37	Teague, Mark. *How I Spent My Summer Vacation.* Decorah, IA: Dragonfly Books, July 8, 1997.
38	Parks, Barbara (author), Brunkus, Denise (illustrator). *Junie B. Jones and a Little Monkey Business.* New York City: Random House Books for Young Readers, November 3, 2010.
39	Muth, Jon J. *The Three Questions (Based on a story by Leo Tolstoy).* New York City: Scholastic, April 1, 2002.
40	dePaola, Tomie. *The Legend of the Indian Paintbrush.* Putnam and Grosset, January 1, 1996.
41	Dr. Seuss. *Oh, The Places You'll Go.* New York City: Random House Books for Young Readers, January 22, 1990.
42	Henkes, Kevin. *Lily's Purple, Plastic Purse.* New York City: Greenwillow, January 1, 2006.

43	Munsch, Robert (author), McGraw, Sheila (illustrator). *Love You Forever.* Ontario, Canada: Firefly Books, September 1, 1995.
44	Carle, Eric. *The Tiny Seed.* New York City: Little Simon, March 10, 2009.
45	Carle, Eric. *The Very Hungry Caterpillar.* Beijing, China: World Publishing Company, 1969.
46	Murphy, Jill. *Five Minutes Peace.* London: Puffin, April 5, 1999.
47	Hoffman, Mary (author), Binch, Caroline (illustrator). *Amazing Grace.* New York City: Dial Books, September 2, 1991.
48	Pinkney, Jerry. *The Lion and the Mouse.* Atlanta, GA: Walker & Company, January 1, 1985.